THE LONG

OF WOMAN'S ...RY

JANE ADDAMS

The Long Road
of Woman's Memory

INTRODUCTION BY
CHARLENE HADDOCK SEIGFRIED

University of Illinois Press
URBANA, CHICAGO, AND SPRINGFIELD

Library of Congress Cataloging-in-Publication Data
Addams, Jane, 1860–1935.
The long road of woman's memory / Jane Addams ;
introduction by Charlene Haddock Seigfried.
p.   cm.
Includes bibliographical references and index.
ISBN 0-252-02709-4 (cloth : alk. paper)/ISBN 978-0-252-02709-3
ISBN 0-252-07024-0 (paper : alk. paper)/ISBN 978-0-252-07024-2
1. Women—Psychology. 2. Women—History.
I. Seigfried, Charlene Haddock, 1943– . II. Title.
HQ1206.A25   2002
305.4'09—dc21   2001002293

To My Dear Friend
Mary H. Wilmarth
Whose Memory Stored with the Best in Literature
and Whose Fine Public Spirit Are Daily Placed
at the Service of Her Friends and of Her City,
with a Gallant and Gentle Courtesy

Contents

Introduction to the
Illinois Edition

CHARLENE HADDOCK SEIGFRIED

If Jane Addams had accomplished only a small fraction of what she actually did, she would still deserve a place in our memories. Taken all together, her accomplishments make her not only one of the outstanding women of her time but also of any time. Addams first became a national figure through her work at the Hull-House settlement in Chicago, which she founded along with Ellen Gates Starr in 1889. Working together with an unusually dedicated, creative, and effective group of women, she was instrumental in developing a cooperative rather than positivistic social science approach to the enormous problems generated by laissez-faire capitalism.[1] She helped found the first kindergarten, playground, and juvenile court system in Chicago and was active on a wide range of social issues, from the emancipation of women to public hygiene. Among the urban social issues that concerned Addams and the first-generation residents Florence Kelley, Julia Lathrop, Dr. Alice Hamilton, and Starr were "compulsory education, child labor, mothers' pensions, parks and playgrounds, workmen's compensation, vocational education and guidance, protection of newly arrived immigrants, women's labor unions, and crusades against prostitution."[2]

Over the years, Addams's interests expanded outward from Chicago to the nation and the world. She "was a member of the first executive committee of the National Association for the Advancement of Colored People, a vice-president of the National American Woman Suffrage Association, and a founder of the American Union Against Militarism, from which emerged both the Foreign Policy Association and the American Civil Liberties Union. She was elected chairman of the Woman's Peace Party in 1915, and in 1919 became the first president of the Woman's International League for Peace and Freedom, having presided over the 1915 International Congress of Women at The Hague from which the league originated."[3] She was also an accomplished speaker and prolific author, with ten books and more than five hundred articles and book chapters to her credit.

The Long Road of Woman's Memory was originally published in 1916 when Addams was fifty-six. It was written while she was recuperating from a long illness and an operation removing one of her kidneys. It was also the beginning of a time of deep discouragement and growing isolation because of her continuing efforts for peace while war raged in Europe. Following the zenith of her worldwide preeminence after the publication of *Twenty Years at Hull-House,* her popularity began to plummet as her patriotism came under increasing attack by the media.[4] The originality and power of Addams's contributions to pragmatist philosophy are strikingly evident in *The Long Road of Woman's Memory,* which she liked best among her work after *The Spirit of Youth and the City Streets.*[5] It is true that some aspects of her writings are dated, as would be expected in any intellectual endeavor that deals with contemporary issues, and does not take refuge in abstract universals and safe platitudes that exclude actual conditions and popular understanding. But many of her beliefs and judgments remain fresh and challenging, not least the very invocation of specific memories of actual women as a basis for philosophic reflection and socially transformative action.

From the perspective of contemporary feminist theory, I initially found Addams's book puzzling and a little disappointing. I had expected to be introduced to eminent and interesting women who had preceded Addams and influenced her life and ideas. I had also hoped that she would develop some worthwhile arguments for why retrieving them from oblivion was so important. In other words, I expected to find a hitherto ignored predecessor to current feminist work in rediscovering and reevaluating the neglected work of earlier women activists and thinkers. The recovery of foremothers was conceived of as a revolutionary act at the beginning of the current women's movement, and their lives and writing became the focus of many books.[6] One surprising discovery was that over the centuries women were constantly rediscovering their 'lost' history and that it seemed vitally important to do so.[7]

Simone de Beauvoir shrewdly explained why in *The Second Sex* when she said that women have not overthrown their subordination because they have not yet learned to say 'we.' Found throughout every strata and division of society, they lack concrete means for forming themselves into a cohesive unit corresponding to men's solidarity of power. "They have no past, no history, no religion of their own" that would give them a perspective through which their common interests could become apparent.[8]

That bleak assessment is no longer true. Not surprisingly, as women's studies and feminist theory have gained a foothold in colleges and universities, scholarly retrievals of women's lives and accomplishments have proliferated. We now have access to many centuries of women's grievances, legal prohibitions, and lesser status on the one hand and outstanding achievements and writings on the other hand. The recovery of women's history has become more extensive in scope, simultaneously less parochial and more specialized and more sensitive to the theoretical issues examined.[9]

Instead of such forays into the past, Addams plumbs the memories of her own contemporaries. They are ordinary women whom she has encountered over the course of her life and are drawn from all classes, although most are poor or from the working class. Once again, her choice of subject differs from the early works of the recent feminist wave. Robin Morgan's *Sisterhood Is Powerful,* for example, sought to make more widely available and preserve for posterity contemporary speeches, manifestos, and other writings of leaders of the women's liberation movement.[10] Even though Addams did not meet my initial expectations, my curiosity was aroused. What was "the long road" if not the retrievable works of earlier generations of literate, politically active, controversial women? Just what was it about "women's memories" that struck her as important enough to write about? In what follows, I will explore her unique angle of vision on women's memories in the belief that she has some genuinely new insights to contribute to contemporary theory.

By appealing specifically to women's memories, it becomes apparent that most philosophical discussions of memory, whether in the context of the philosophy of mind, of epistemology, or of philosophical psychology, commit the rationalist fallacy (or the fallacy of misplaced concreteness). The glaring exception is found in Jewish discussions of Shoah, the Holocaust, which often include theories of memory tied to that specific event and its aftermath. According to William James, the rationalist fallacy is the habit of abstracting ideas from experience and then opposing these simplified concepts to the complexity of lived experience, which is thereby distorted. Likewise, for John Dewey, processes in the fallacy of misplaced concreteness are converted into antecedent existences. Such a reified term as *memory* is then supposed to delimit actual processes of memory. Whatever does not fit the essentialist model is denied, falsified, or ignored. What remains is then elevated to the status of eternal or necessary truth. On the occasion of the 250th anniversary of Johann Wolfgang von Goethe's birth, for example, Jochen Hieber praised as one of his great achievements the fact that "like no other German writer Goethe became a creative metamorphoser, transforming his own life into poetry, transforming existing reality into timeless valid statements." Goethe has indeed transformed his subjective experiences into sublime literature that has stood the test of time. But can any one man's life, no matter how intensely lived and no matter how brilliant the artistic expression, depict, as Hieber claims, "all of life's phases while at the same time being a model for all stages of existence"?[11]

In contrast to the model of the self as all-encompassing and exemplary memory as the prerogative of genius, Addams sought in her autobiographical accounts, beginning with *Twenty Years at Hull-House,* to understand herself and others as transformed and challenged through interactions, among which memories seemed to play a dynamic role. She founded a settlement house in the overcrowded, immigrant, working-class district of Chicago in the midst of the poverty, unsanitary conditions, and political corruption that the industrial revolution spawned. She explained her decision as an attempt to "learn of life from life itself" rather than at second hand.[12] One way she learned from life was by respecting those she wanted to help enough to listen to what they had to say and then reflect on what their insights and memories contributed to better understanding the pressing problems making their lives so miserable. In one case, she seeks out and recounts the reminiscences of working women, whose memories integrated their individual experiences with more impersonal aspects of life. What surprises her is not their ability to relate concrete experiences to more generalized meanings but rather that such fructifying aspects of memory can occur—even in the limited circumstances of industrialized poverty and the lack of formal education. Whether or not surprise reflected her actual state of mind at the time, alluding to the surprising character of the finding called attention to a fact that the upper and middle classes did not want to admit: Recent working-class immigrants had something of value to contribute to human understanding.

The word *memory*, as used in most contemporary philosophical discourse, has no gender, ethnicity, or class; in pragmatist terms, it lacks context.[13] If "neglect of context is the greatest single disaster which philosophic thinking can incur," then the disastrous results of contemporary reflections on memory should be evident and could be the subject of further demonstration.[14] Addams's contextually rich method is amply exemplified in *The Long Road of Woman's Memory*. Despite the impression given by a use of language typical of her time in the title, Addams is not thinking of an archetype of 'woman' in place of individual women or of a disembodied essence of memory rather than of specific memories. Her chapter titles, for example, pluralize both terms—"Women's Memories." Along with other pragmatists, Addams debunks the myth of an essential human nature or feminine nature, often appealing instead to her experience of living in the midst of groups of recent immigrants "whose history, language and customs show the tremendous variability of human nature."[15]

Addams has been accused of believing in an essential feminine nature, but it is more accurate to say that she believed that some of the experiences women shared (such as bearing children) were unique to them and gave them a particular angle of vision. Like Charlotte Perkins Gilman, she thought women were more inclined to sympathetic understanding, pacifism, and cooperativeness than men. Unlike Gilman, she believed that these traits were due to the differing roles society expected women and men to play, roles she challenged in her life and writing. She also believed that to the extent that the particular needs of women, arising from their circumstances, could be raised to consciousness, they could be tapped as a revolutionary force for change. Because "political action should concern itself with genuine human needs," women had a stake in the political process in order to create "a better world for their children to live in."[16]

Along with many examples of the cross-cultural similarities of women's interests, she also reports that the looked-for pacifism that feminists expected of the first women elected to Congress after receiving the vote never materialized. Although women could possibly become a revolutionary force by bringing a new perspective to politics, one that would not be afraid to change in relationship to social and political changes, they instead "demonstrated that it is much easier to dovetail into the political schemes of men than to release the innate concerns of women."[17] Such concerns are only innate in the sense that they have arisen in response to particular circumstances, such as the worldwide phenomenon of being given the care of young children, not in the sense of being genetically programmed or unchangeable. There is a difference between what pragmatists call "generic traits of experience" or "concrete universals" and universal essences.

The various aspects of memory that Addams explores are derived from how some women use their memories to explain their beliefs and actions. Their use of memory is interpreted dialogically, with Addams as a sympathetic and intellectually astute partner in the dialogue. The women's stories provide the context for reflective analysis; they do not merely illustrate an independent position. This is not to imply that Addams does not bring to the situation her own interests and perspectives that lead her to emphasize some features of the context rather than others. She emphasizes the ways in which memory is not merely passive recall but a dynamic factor in making sense of often painful experiences and radically changing one's core beliefs in the process.

Memory, according to Addams in the Introduction, has two functions, which can operate independently or be mutually transformative (p. 5). In the first instance, memory works as an interpreter of experience and tends to recast the episodic events of the past into a more harmonious, self-appeasing pattern. Second, it acts as a selective agency in social reorganization. In both cases, memory is highly selective even though subjectively experienced as simple, unbiased reportage.

Addams's methodology has affinities with core pragmatist positions. William James explains truth as the marriage of old opinion to new fact with a minimum of jolt and a maximum of continuity.[18] The person involved is the judge of whether or not the marriage is satisfactory. Such is the hold of settled beliefs that if something happens to call them into question we tend to either ignore the counter-evidence as long as we can or abuse those who point out such disturbing possibilities. Truth grows when it sometimes happens that events cannot be ignored but that beliefs need to be altered in order to deal with new facts.

Likewise for Dewey, maintaining the continuity of knowing with activities that purposely modify the environment is the essential feature of the pragmatic theory of method. "Only that which has been organized into our disposition so as to enable us to adapt the environment to our needs and to adapt our aims and desires to the situation in which we live is really knowledge." Such organized dispositions are encoded in memory but not as a static deposit: "Knowledge as an act is bringing some of our dispositions to consciousness with a view to straightening out a perplexity, by conceiving the connection between ourselves and the world in which we live."[19] The means Addams uses to encourage reminiscences creatively express what Dewey took to be the heart of communication: "the establishment of cooperation in an activity in which there are partners, and in which the activity of each is modified and regulated by partnership."[20]

In *Twenty Years at Hull-House*, Addams gives one of the first accounts of the conflicts between first and second generations of immigrants, discord that contributed to the crime, family disintegration, and juvenile delinquency in the tenements of Chicago. She urges the use of a dynamic educational process, one Dewey explained as "a continuing reconstruction of experience," as a way of bridging the tensions between the generations. She immediately couples that approach with "reverence of the past which Goethe declares to be the basis for all sound progress."[21] Daughters could be led to admire their mothers instead of being embarrassed about them if they could learn to recognize the value, beauty, and continuity of their mother's handwork. The newly Americanized second generation often perceived as old-fashioned such Old World skills as weaving and sewing traditional clothing. First-generation immigrant mothers, for their part, could learn to take pride in their accomplishments instead of being bewildered by new surroundings and demoralized by the prejudice they experienced.

More is involved than bringing to consciousness, revaluing, and preserving past ways of life, however. Immigrant parents too often contributed to alienating their offspring by the exercise of harsh patriarchal authority. Many had immigrated from impoverished rural communities and had minimal education. They, too, had to learn to value what their children were learning from new experiences in an industrialized society.

The pragmatist appeal to knowledge as the outcome of experience is a central feature of Addams's philosophy. But she is also very aware that it takes courage to learn from experience and there are many obstacles to doing so. She listed some in 1930 to explain why women had not yet followed through with the social reforms expected when they were given the vote. In "Aspects of the Woman's Movement" she observes that she is "quite sure that women in politics thus far have been too conventional, too afraid to differ with the men, too unused to trust to their own judgment, too skeptical of the wisdom of the humble, to release the concern of simple women into the ordering of political life, too inclined to narrow their historic perspective of the experience of the formal woman's movement and thus unwittingly have restricted women's role in the racial development."[22] By not narrowing the memories she retells to those of elite, upper-class women who publicly furthered women's well-being, Addams escapes a frequent criticism of earlier waves of feminism (that the women involved were elitist and class-based) while at the same time developing a model for cultivating experiences that are socially transformative.

Addams does not just rely on the power of memory in *The Long Road of Woman's Memory*. She urges recognition of the organic connection of all strata of society as a central principle of her philosophy. As a consequence, she deliberately and repeatedly calls attention to ties that bind better-off members of society to those at the lower ends of the social ladder so the former will find it in their self-interest to champion members of other classes, religions, ethnic groups, and races being unjustly treated. She points out, for example, that the women's movement demonstrated that the many restrictions oppressing all women under statutory law are directly related to its punitive treatment of the much smaller group of women who bear children out of wedlock. A more recent example of the importance and continued timeliness of the principle of the responsibilities that follow from interconnectedness is the despair of women who have been refugeed by the slaughter in Srebrenica, Yugoslavia. Once they realized that the international community had no intention of doing anything about the event, they turned away from recounting memories of what had happened. Hans Seigfried concurs that without a "strong connection between keeping records of crimes against humanity and protecting the human rights of the living generation . . . mere documentation of crimes committed is simply inhuman."[23]

Each chapter title in *The Long Road of Woman's Memory* emphasizes a creative appropriation of the past. In its transformative possibilities, the use of memory looks to the future rather than repeating what has happened. Perhaps because Addams is interested in the varieties of women's experiences rather than referring to a single, traumatic disaster on the scale of the Holocaust, she does not refer to memory as witness or to bearing witness to trauma. That she emphasizes the salience of the past and memory's more dynamic aspects is evident in her six chapter titles (which also denote thematic content): "Transmuting the Past," "Reacting on Life," "Disturbing Conventions," "Integrating Industry," "Challenging War," and "Interpretative Memory."

According to Dewey, intelligence is the ability to take from present experience something that will be valuable in dealing with future experience.[24] When Addams claimed she got as much from the poor as she was able to give, it was no romantic platitude. It was the expression of a lively intelligence. As part of her sympathetic response to the many old women—often isolated and alone in tenement houses—whom she met during the course of her neighborhood rounds, Addams would engage them in conversation. Not surprisingly, they were more comfortable talking about the past, when they were actively engaged in family affairs and in making a living, rather than about their present dreary situation. But instead of merely passing these reminiscences off as the inevitable result of failing powers, what struck Addams about such encounters was the tendency of the elderly to romanticize their earlier lives. The very real hardships and sorrows they had endured meant that romanticization could not have the same root as a young person's superficially similar tendency to romanticize the world. Addams conjectured that the idealizing transmutation of their experiences must have something to do with a power inherent in memory itself (p. 7).

Her clue was taken from Gilbert Murray's life of Euripides and his explanation of the transforming power of Memory, the mother of the

Muses, who reweaves the delicate fabric of human experience. Already familiar with the romantic fantasies of youth, which she had explained in *The Spirit of Youth,* she applied a similar method for the elderly, whose prosaic lives badly needed such escape.[25] The idea for doing so only became apparent, however, as a result of the bizarre episode of the mythical "Devil Baby," which Addams recounts in not just one but two chapters of *The Long Road of Woman's Memory* and which reappears as a leitmotif throughout the book.[26] Hull-House residents were literally overwhelmed by the power of a widely held superstition to motivate people to nearly hysterical action and ignore and reject more rational explanations. Their first reactions were like Dewey's toward folktales; he explained in a discussion of memory, for example, that "students of the primitive history of mankind tell of the enormous part played by animal tales, myths and cults."[27] But Addams's constant practice of reflecting on experience and learning from it, especially experience that was perplexing because it could not be assimilated into her own stock of beliefs, soon led her to a strikingly different assessment.[28]

Addams's belief that older people, especially older women, are an underused and precious resource is not one that is widely shared. She admits to dropping whatever she was doing at Hull-House and rushing off to hear old women talk whenever an opportunity arose. She seems to have been inspired to write about memory by the fact that elderly people who are denied active participation in day-to-day affairs tend to live more in the past than the present. What makes poor, displaced, elderly women's reminiscences bearable, it seems to Addams, is that they transmute the past rather than simply recall it. In doing so, the memory of the pain and misery of earlier years appears to provide comfort rather than bitterness. Addams's sympathetic understanding of elderly women, and her ability to gain valuable insights about memory from interacting with them, contrasts with Dewey's more anthropological approach that emphasizes the disjunction between ways of life and modern civilization. Where Addams recognizes the therapeutic effect of romanticizing an otherwise unbearable past, Dewey sees an earlier stage of development. "Since [early] man revives his past experience because of the interest added to what would otherwise be the emptiness of present leisure," he observes, "the primitive life of memory is one of fancy and imagination, rather than of accurate recollection."[29] Dewey also attributes the dramatic recreation and re-imagining of the past to the leisure that primitive man enjoyed when not actively engaged in hunting or fishing expeditions. By focusing on the memories of contemporary women and how myth functioned in their lives, Addams develops a competing explanation.

Addams illustrates the power of memory to transmute the past by an incident that began when three Italian women excitedly rushed through the Hull-House door and demanded to see the Devil Baby. They graphically described a baby in the form of a devil, complete with cloven hooves, tail, and pointed ears, and would not believe residents' denials that no such baby existed. For six weeks, people of all walks of life and education from across the city of Chicago deluged the settlement day and night, demanding to see the demonic baby. Addams and the other workers soon heard hundreds of variations of the tale of the mythic Devil Baby. The Italian version told of an atheist husband who had torn down his pious wife's holy picture from the wall and said he would sooner have a devil in the house than such an image. When their baby was born, he was indeed a tiny devil who ran about shaking his finger accusingly at his father. The Jewish version, again with many variations of detail, has the father announcing before the birth of a seventh child that he would sooner have a devil in the family than another daughter.

Addams noticed that older women became particularly animated over the Devil Baby. Used to being ignored at home, for a short time they again found themselves in the once-familiar position of enforcing family discipline by describing what would happen if their children disobeyed or their husbands strayed. The rumored actual presence of the Devil Baby at Hull-House gave credence to such moralizing tales. In telling them to Addams, the full tragedy, brutality, and horror of their poverty-stricken lives were revealed at last. One woman's face was permanently twisted, a result of seeing her father stab her mother. Another told of having given birth to fourteen children; the only two who survived were later killed in an explosion. Instead of bitterness, the women seemed to exhibit quiet endurance. Their suffering was not only in the distant past, however. They also told of adult children who beat them for the little money they earned by scrubbing floors, of being bullied and beaten by husbands, and of supporting mentally handicapped or shiftless children.

In hearing the hope and animation in the voices of such old wom-
en (one, a penniless and crippled inmate of a poorhouse, had to be
bodily lifted from the streetcar on her painful journey to Hull-House)
and the disappointment when their hopes were utterly dashed, Addams
found herself tempted to believe with them that the past was much
more important than the present. If such mythic tales of virtue reward-
ed and evil punished were true, then the everyday misery of lives lived
in abject poverty and domestic abuse could be borne with equanimi-
ty. Addams wondered whether the imagination of old age needs to be
fed with folktales, undiminished by warnings that they are untrue, just
as children's imaginations revel in fairy tales.

The vivid interest of so many old women in the story of the Devil
Baby led to Addams's belief that one of the functions of memory is to
transmute the tragic experiences of lives lived in extreme hardship into
something of value. Mothers and grandmothers, alienated from the
lives of the younger generation born in America, bemoaned the fact
that no one in the family any longer paid attention to them. It was evident "that the old women who came to visit the Devil Baby believed
that the story would secure them a hearing at home" (pp. 15–16). Even
more than such vain efforts to regain a sense of importance and dig-
nity, what impressed Addams was memory's power to sift and recon-
cile the inconsistencies and perplexities of life, to transmute the dross
of disappointments into emotional serenity.

The more she thought about it, the more evident it became to Addams that experience eventually is nothing but memory and that a
powerful way to make experience useful to further experiences is to
encapsulate its lessons metaphorically. Dewey also notes that experience, lived through and moment to moment, is too taken up with the
task at hand to be fully conscious and human. "Only later [when a
person resurveys all the moments in thought] do the details compose
into a story and fuse into a whole of meaning."[30] Although curiosity
played a part, Addams says that many visitors to the Devil Baby "prized
the story as a valuable instrument in the business of living" (p. 17). Their
eagerness to learn the exact details of how the Devil Baby was born and
came to reside at Hull-House—and the skepticism often exhibited at
the strange reluctance of residents to show the baby or make money
by exhibiting it—recalled a process by which legends might have been

born, evolved, and cherished over centuries. For women, the Devil Baby had special significance as a means to chastise the abusive husbands and fathers often brought along to view it by their wives and daughters. These men showed palpable relief when no demonic baby could be produced.

Addams anticipates later feminist theories of women's hidden contributions to literature evident in such titles as "Anonymous was a Woman" when she speculates that women invented fairy tales as moral parables of reward and retribution. How else could they protect themselves from husbands angry that they have given birth only to female babies? Addams points out that we are still under the influence of such traditional stories: "They remind us that for thousands of years women had nothing to oppose against unthinkable brutality save 'the charm of words,' no other implement with which to subdue the fierce-nesses of the world about them." It is not too far-fetched to suspect that to protect vulnerable children and secure a measure of pity for themselves, "the obscure victims of unspeakable wrong and brutality, have embodied their memories in a literature of their own" (p. 19).

Addams argues for the central pragmatist principle that "new knowledge derived from concrete experience is continually being made available for the guidance of human life" (p. 19). But the kind of knowledge derived, and the nature of the concrete experience drawn on, represents a radically new voice in pragmatist philosophy. By going beyond the seeming gullibility and ignorance exhibited in the episode of the Devil Baby and paying attention to some of the most marginalized members of society, taking seriously their desires and needs, she concludes, "Humble women are still establishing rules of conduct as best they may, to counteract the base temptations of a man's world" (p. 19). Literally hundreds of women were attracted to the story of the Devil Baby. Its direct—indeed, fantastic—link between wrong-doing and punishment reflected their longing to make sense of their own experiences as recent immigrants to an often dangerous and unsettling urban environment. It particularly seemed to provide a way for women to discuss the abuses they suffered in a society and culture dominated by men whose own explanations of their behavior distorted or denied rather than clarified women's experiences. The second chapter of *The Long Road of Woman's Memory,* for example, is filled with descriptions of the shockingly miserable lives of women who lived in the vicinity of Hull-House. There had been a premature birth caused by the baby's father kicking its pregnant mother in her side, children had been maimed and burned because there was no one to leave them with when both parents were at work, and babies died because their fathers would not allow their mothers to send for a doctor.

The catalyst for the insights that inform her book on women's memories, however, was one that ran counter to the Euripidean clue that memory reconciles one to life. To her surprise, another function of memory became apparent, its power to disturb society by challenging existing conventions (chapter 3). For Addams, women tend to be swayed by the past because of tradition, which makes it all the more remarkable when they challenge settled conventions. She also observed that although a woman's experience may lead her to engage in social reconstruction, she can also count on many other women whose motherly instincts will lead them to recognize and oppose social injustices. In fact, Addams asserts, the masses of women and men are more likely sources of great social changes than are the intellectuals who articulate them.

Addams's seemingly casual, oblique invocation of William James's focus on concrete, everyday experience as the origin of philosophical reflection for pragmatists indicates the importance she attaches to his doctrine of selective interest. According to James's radically empiricist philosophy, sensory stimuli do not passively imprint reality on our neurons and brain, but we actively select the aspects of the environment that interest us and ignore most of what is available.[31] In so doing, we cooperatively bring about a meaningful world in which we can feel at home. What we take to be reality is a dynamic interplay among inherited beliefs, interests, and needs and what we encounter. Using James's doctrine of selective interest to organize her experiences, what surprised Addams (and struck her as aggressively modern) was that the vital power of selection she saw at work in the reminiscences of some elderly women did not force the women's beliefs onto present experience, as had happened in the case of the Devil Baby. Instead, in their reminiscences they softened the harsh realities of the past in a way that ran counter to the conventions and traditions that are commonly believed to dominate older minds.

Addams at once recognized the politically radical potential of such transformations. Besides explaining truths as the marriage of past beliefs to present events, James also said that everything is in flux and nothing is foreordained. Often new events are assimilated into old beliefs and nothing changes. At other times, however, past beliefs give way, and new truths—and, consequently, new arrangements of reality—emerge. Addams postulates that such rearrangements are most likely to occur when conventions are being challenged and discarded and conformists are forced to defend their beliefs against those who would destroy them. Women can then find themselves forced by personal circumstances to reassert the values of family life against their own narrowly moralistic judgments. Addams gives as an example a widow whose husband had been killed in unsavory circumstances. The woman had come to see that her excessively rigid moral code had contributed to her only son's suicide after he had supposedly fathered a child out of wedlock. It gradually dawned on her that to reproach the dissolute woman responsible, even as she agreed to take her and her son into her home and care for them, was likely to lead to a repetition of the tragic events in the next generation. The young woman left and went back to her old ways, but the widow, aware of her own unwitting complicity in the tragedy, realized that to condemn her as a moral failure did not do justice to the complexity of the situation. Not even her subsequent realization that the "grandchild" she had agreed to raise was not her son's child led her to retract her new view of reality and altered sense of what justice requires.

Addams reports that further conversations with the widow showed that the woman was aware of using her memories, her repeated reflections on the past, to achieve a new sense of social values and changed attitudes toward a class of women she had formerly condemned (p. 33). She realized that the intolerance of supposedly respectable women toward so-called fallen women made them jointly responsible for the very acts they deplored. They were more concerned with assuaging their pride than seeing that justice was done. It is impossible to determine how much Addams learned about the widow's thought processes and attitudes and how much she contributed to altering them. Such ambiguity is inherent in the give-and-take of conversations that often lead to conclusions jointly arrived at. Addams's pragmatist feminism is exhibited in her preference for expressing her insights as the outcome of dialogues with others. That she shaped the beliefs of others is evident when she remarks that the moralistic pride the widow acknowledges erects barricades to such shared dialogues by "deliberately shutting out sympathetic understanding" (p. 33). The disapprobation this is meant to convey can only be fully grasped in the context of Addams's theory about sympathetic understanding being central to obtaining both accurate knowledge and better values.[32]

It is also her intention to be explicit in drawing a connection between individual experiences and widespread social movements. Addams stresses the continuity between mothers' remembered love and concern for their children, who needed to be nourished and cherished in order to properly grow and develop, and the need under changed industrial conditions to extend similar protective care to those children born out of wedlock and their mothers. She argues that the organized women's movement grew out of such revolts against gross injustices. The movement's achievements "demonstrate that woman deals most efficiently with fresh experiences when she coalesces them into the impressions Memory has kept in store for her. Eagerly seeking continuity with the past by her own secret tests of affinity, she reinforces and encourages Memory's instinctive processes of selection" (p. 41). It is not accidental that the widow's change of heart concerning illegitimacy is used to illustrate the role of memory. An important goal of the woman's movement at the time was to challenge prevailing moral judgments and revise the legal code in regard to unwed mothers and their children. Therefore, as a deliberate means of changing conventional attitudes, Addams reconceptualizes the way some old beliefs are married to new facts.

Addams opens the fourth chapter of *The Long Road of Woman's Memory*, "Integrating Industry," by alluding to the pragmatist theory of knowledge. According to that theory, concrete universals originate in particular experiences. From them, beliefs are formed that—through further testing—are found to be applicable to a wider range of experiences. These beliefs, now formulated as judgments, only become genuinely universal insofar as they are confirmed by others in relevant situations. Addams typically develops her insights into the nature of knowledge by first elevating the story of the Devil Baby to an epistemologically relevant status, treating it as an example of just such an attempt to generalize from experience. She explicitly links it to the mission usually attributed only to higher literature, that of translating particular acts into ones of universal significance. Addams's radical revision of the tradition is evident in her reinterpretation of a story intellectuals judge as an example of the grossest superstition. To those who would reduce its significance by limiting its provenance to that of a few ignorant women immigrants, Addams slyly points out that the tale was told by "simple, hardworking women who at any given moment compose the bulk of the women in the world" (p. 43).

Unlike Charles Sanders Peirce's invocation of elite scientists as the best exemplars and practitioners of the search for knowledge, Dewey always emphasized the continuity between everyday ways of resolving problematic situations and more formal theories of inquiry. Among the pragmatists, only Addams concretely demonstrates what ordinary women have contributed to human understanding and how they did so. She draws attention to her transgressive aim by expressing surprise that it is working-class women in the harshest, most monotonous, industrial circumstances who have used their memories to successfully integrate individual experiences with broader, more impersonal insights (p. 43). In chapter 4, Addams demonstrates that thesis by recounting what she heard in many conversations with working-class women. She describes how they managed to develop a new sense of values from the tragic conditions of their lives. Their memories of suffering were allies in breaking down the widespread stigma against unionization, giving them insight into the injustices of industrialization and the courage to organize or to join unions, often at great cost to themselves.

Reflecting on a meeting that took place during a Garment Workers strike, Addams recalls the episode of the Devil Baby to express the overwhelming waste of women's unused capacity. By noting that they sat in the same chairs as their mothers did during the Devil Baby incident, she connects the stubborn endurance of the young women on strike with that of their mothers. The responses of both generations were rooted in human affections, yet, she argues, there was a significant difference in the way endurance was expressed. The young women could not renew their motivations through such emotions as the maternal love that motivated their mothers in caring for them when they were ill, nor were they naturally attracted to the objects of their sacrifices. Their feminine impulses and affections were not used in the alienating conditions of their industrialized jobs. Factory workers engaged in repetitive activities could not see the outcome of their labors or the connection between one area of work and the improvement of a more encompassing situation. Women working at home did, however, in regard to their labors and the overall welfare of their families.

But Addams does not nostalgically call for a return to the home. Through their organizing efforts with different nationalities, she notes, the working classes forge new bonds absolutely unlike family bonds. Instead of using traditional skills, young women "for the first time in the long history of women's labor, are uniting their efforts in order to obtain opportunities for a fuller and more normal living" (p. 49). Unlike women limited to domestic labor, they possess the enormous advantage "of having experienced the discipline arising from impersonal obligations and of having tasted the freedom from economic dependence, so valuable that too heavy a price can scarcely be paid for it" (p. 50).

Addams knows that such uncompromising declarations alarm the more conservative elements of society. She recalls that it has been predicted from time immemorial that a war of the sexes will be unleashed in the clash between the traditional view that women's duties should be restricted to family obligations and their more complex obligations under conditions such as industrialization. Yet Addams denies the accusation that when oppressed women strike back they will do so out of the revenge of madness rather than a sense of justice. Wryly, she notes that she never witnessed such a mood among women active in the labor movement, a contention she backs with a recollection of a woman who organized the garment trades.

Because memories suppress or blur nonessentials and myriads of details, Addams thinks that common human experiences are thereby thrown into high relief. In chapter 5, she offers as evidence the two months she spent in Europe during 1915, when some women she encountered had lost house, home, and children. They talked not of recriminations but rather of the way that war had destroyed such basic human relations that it must not be thought of as an acceptable recourse for nations. Addams also shows how memory functions in "Challenging War." She makes her usual argument: Women, who are responsible for giving life, will find the violent and systematic taking of life abhorrent. They will be drawn to pacifism and can become its most effective leaders. She approaches the issue by drawing on the memories of two women on opposite sides during the "great European war" (World War I) and shows how, despite differences in country, class, and education, they came to the same conclusion as to the folly of war. For Addams, the issue is one of a long series of moral revolutions in which a cherished custom is revalued as wrong. Human consciousness has reached the same stage of sensitiveness in regard to war as it did earlier in regard to human sacrifice. She concludes by calling on women to align themselves with those at the bottom of society who are ever-oppressed, "the suffering mothers of the disinherited," and listen to their own "haunting memories" (p. 67) as women, who, as the nurturers of life, should instinctively challenge war as the implacable enemy of life.

Addams draws most explicitly on women's maternal instincts when she writes about pacifism. But even in these stories, she is careful to relate women's feelings and attitudes to specific experiences, such as giving birth and caring for children.[33] Any such deeply felt aspects of experience would influence beliefs and conduct, according to pragmatists. For contemporary pragmatist feminists, even allowing for the possibility of sexual differences based on the existence of differences in genital, chromosomal, and hormonal factors, gendered nature is acquired only over time and through the way the interplay of personal needs and attitudes with social interactions develops or stunts such factors.[34] Neither does Addams naively assume that all women are nurturant by nature or that a natural maternal instinct inevitably leads to opposing war. She demonstrates instead that beliefs arise and change through recollections and reflections and that original feelings become transformed into new attitudes and actions through a dynamic process of memory in the face of challenging circumstances. She believes that in the cultures of her time—where behavior, social roles, employment, and other social standards were strongly divided along sexual as well as class and ethnic lines—women and other oppressed groups shared traits that predisposed them to pacifism. Her speeches and organizing activities are therefore directed toward convincing women of a relationship between their typically female experiences and a radical theory of opposition to established authority, patriotic tradition, and military supremacy.

After five chapters, each introduced by the words "Women's Memories" and followed by the specific function of memory to be considered in dialogue with those through whom the themes arose, the last chapter breaks the pattern and abruptly shifts focus. Chapter 6 is called "A Personal Experience in Interpretative Memory." Instead of elaborating yet another aspect of her deeply contextualized theory of memory (in this instance its interpretive function), Addams reminisces about her childhood fears and reflects on death. In the introduction, she acknowledges that this chapter's only link with those preceding it is that they all have something to do with memory. In addition, she almost apologizes for including her personal experiences in the book (p. 6). Neither claim does her justice, however. After having sympathetically responded to the memories of women of many ethnicities and classes and acted as mediator between their individual experiences and wider social issues, it is typical of Addams to share something of herself with them. In a dialogue, it would be rude not to.

It has been said that because we all experience death, the neglect of that theme by pragmatists is a weakness in their theory.[35] Once again, Addams is the exception. She writes about memories within memories, recalling her thoughts about death occasioned by a trip to Egypt that brought up childhood memories of death. Both sets of memories were recalled as a way of dealing with the effects of war during what she calls a "cataclysmic summer in Europe" in 1915 (p. 5). Stylistically, however, the chapter does not fit well with what came before, and Addams unwittingly demonstrates the awkwardness of inserting the existentialist theme of living toward death into the framework of a philosophy focused on life.

Addams cryptically mentions that the process of memory in the last chapter reverses what she had said about it in the first two. It is not clear what she meant. It could be that whereas she had been showing how women used their memories to transmute the inconsistencies and perplexities of life into an emotional serenity (chapter 1, p. 16), or used their memories "as a valuable instrument in the business of living" (chapter 2, p. 17), Addams's visit to the archeological sites of Egypt first called up and then soothed her childhood fears of death. In other words, present experiences allowed her to put to rest earlier fearful memories rather than mull them over until they changed the present. She was interpreting "racial and historic experiences through personal reminiscences" (p. 68) rather than the reverse. Or, perhaps she meant that although (until the last chapter) she had stressed the diverse ways memory recalls the past because memories are dynamic, selective, and transformative, what most struck her was a sense of the continuity of past and present, of adult fears with those of childhood, and of the strategies of consolation individuals developed to deal with the inevitability of death.

Unlike Addams's recounting of the tale of the Devil Baby (where she described the power women wrest from what others denigrate as primitive superstition), in chapter 6 she uncritically accepts the judgment that ancient cultures are primitive in comparison to contemporary Western cultures, as untutored, naturally primitive young children are compared to their adult state. The entire chapter is organized according to a trope that equates the intellectual processes and emotions of early childhood with the equally primitive level of thinking and artistic expression characteristic of earlier stages of human development. Addams's childishly "primitive emotion" of the fear of death, for example, is vividly revived in the presence of ancient funeral art, which she perceives as both childishly executed in a "very primitive style of drawing" (p. 69) and an irrational attempt to wall out death by means of magic tricks.

Through reflecting on the recurring "ghosts of reminiscence" that characterized her travels in Egypt, Addams muses that primitive terror at the dissolution of the body gradually gives way to calm acceptance of death as a necessary part of the order of the universe. She also rejects the denigration of the primitive as something to be left behind in a more enlightened age. For her, the wisdom of a "new humanism" consists in its understanding that no myth that consoled earlier generations can lose all significance for later generations. She ends the chapter by stressing the continuity of the lives of modern Egyptian villagers with those of our own and extolling "an almost mystical sense of the life common to all the centuries" (p. 79). In explicitly linking the time she and her special friend Mary Rozet Smith spent in Egypt with the story of the Devil Baby in *The Second Twenty Years at Hull-House,*

Addams emphasizes the acquisition of "a new sense of the unending effort of women throughout the earth that human life might be maintained upon its surface."[36] Despite her equation of childishness with primitivism in earlier eras, she leaves no doubt that she is convinced of the equal worth and importance of all people.

Drawing upon the pragmatic evolutionary principle that old values are rejected and new values arise through selective interests, Addams emphasizes that dawning social struggles are composed from inchoate beginnings of selective memories that subtly alter traditions. Over the years, she encountered many women whose experiences of family relationships or of the labor market led them to modify their conduct so it diverged from accepted norms and contributed toward developing a new standard. Enough such deviation eventually leads to new norms.

As these women recounted their lives to the sympathetic Addams, they unconsciously disclosed the monstrous social injustices responsible for the harsh lives they had endured. Addams quickly recognized the potential for consciousness-raising and social revolution in these disclosures when she noted that mutual reminiscences reveal the commonality of some significant experiences among people who are otherwise so disparate. As the past undergoes transformation in recital, social changes begin to take shape. Reformers can formulate more explicitly the relation between personally harsh experiences and social injustices and accelerate the process of transforming present conditions into a more just social order.

Addams's interest in women's memories is thoroughly pragmatist and at the same time extends in new directions.[37] She adds a new dimension to a rich pragmatist tradition in which memory is not simple recall but a new, constituting act of consciousness. Her practice agrees with Dewey's theory of knowledge: "While the content of knowledge is what *has* happened, what is taken as finished and hence settled and sure, the *reference* of knowledge is future or prospective. For knowledge furnishes the means of understanding or giving meaning to what is still going on and what is to be done."[38] Addams constantly draws upon a fund of personal experience to reach theoretical conclusions and is vigilant about consulting the experiences of others before deciding which practical steps should be taken to remedy present ills and injustices. She thus liberates pragmatist methodology once and for all from a too-literal connection with science. Her work exemplifies what Dewey called "an ideally perfect knowledge," one that "would represent such a network of interconnections that any past experience would offer a point of advantage from which to get at the problem presented in a new experience."[39]

Dewey begins his genealogy of philosophy in one of his most radical books, *Reconstruction in Philosophy*, by asserting that human beings differ from lower animals because we preserve our experiences. He shows how the selectivity of memory and the monopoly of tradition by dominant, upper-class male rulers accounts for the blind spots that have led philosophers to dismiss the contributions of the poor and slaves to the development of knowledge.[40] Addams's *Long Road of Woman's Memory* also reveals the selectivity of memory and challenges its one-sided concentration of power and the monopoly of tradition and knowledge by a privileged few. Only by continuing along the same road (and extending it in new directions) will conventional blind spots to the experiences and contributions of post-colonialist people and suppressed or disregarded minorities be overcome.

NOTES

1. Eleanor J. Stebner, *The Women of Hull House: A Study in Spirituality, Vocation, and Friendship* (Albany: State University of New York Press, 1997); Mary Jo Deegan, *Jane Addams and the Men of the Chicago School, 1892–1918* (New Brunswick: Transaction Books, 1988); Kathryn Kish Sklar, "Hull-House Maps and Papers: Social Science as Women's Work in the 1890s," in *Gender and American Social Science: The Formative Years*, ed. Helene Silverberg (Princeton: Princeton University Press, 1998).

2. Lynn D. Gordon, *Gender and Higher Education in the Progressive Era* (New Haven: Yale University Press, 1990), 89.

3. Ellen Condliffe Lagemann, Introduction to *Jane Addams on Education* (New York: Teachers College Press, 1985), 30.

4. James Weber Linn, *Jane Addams* (1935, repr. Urbana: University of Illinois Press, 1990), 258–59. During this time of increasing media attacks, Addams acerbically remarked that the freedom of the press meant "the freedom to misinterpret any statement they do not like, and to suppress any statement they do not understand." Quoted in Linn, *Jane Addams*, 324.

5. Ibid., 321.

6. Among such books are Leslie B. Tanner, ed., *Voices from Women's Liberation* (New York: New American Library, 1970); Alice S. Rossi, ed., *The Feminist Papers: From Addams to de Beauvoir* (New York: Columbia University Press, 1973); James L. Cooper and Sheila M. Cooper, eds., *The Roots of American Feminist Thought* (Boston: Allyn and Bacon, 1973); and Mary Anne Warren, *The Nature of Woman: An Encyclopedia and Guide to the Literature* (Inverness, Calif.: Edgepress, 1980).

7. Dale Spender, *Women of Ideas (and What Men Have Done to Them)* (London: Ark Paperbacks, 1983).

8. Simone de Beauvoir, *The Second Sex,* ed. H. M. Parshley (New York: Vintage Books, 1974), xxii.

9. See, for example, Sally Gregory Kohlstedt, ed., *History of Women in the Sciences* (Chicago: University of Chicago Press, 1999).

10. Robin Morgan, ed., *Sisterhood Is Powerful: An Anthology of Writings from the Women's Liberation Movement* (New York: Vintage Books, 1970).

11. Jochen Hieber, "Giant of German Literature Johann Wolfgang von Goethe's 250th Anniversary," *Deutschland* 99 (June–July 1999): 52–57.

12. Jane Addams, *Twenty Years at Hull-House* (Urbana: University of Illinois Press, 1990), 72. Besides Addams's own account of the founding and development of the Hull-House settlement, see also Mina Carson, *Settlement Folk: Social Thought and the American Settlement Movement, 1885–1930* (Chicago: University of Chicago Press, 1990).

13. At most, the context is a history of ideas within philosophy itself, as in John Sutton, *Philosophy and Memory Traces: Descartes to Connectionism* (New York: Cambridge University Press, 1998).

14. John Dewey, *Context and Thought,* included in Dewey, *Later Works,* vol. 6: *1931–32,* ed. Jo Ann Boydston (Carbondale: Southern Illinois University Press, 1985), 11.

15. Jane Addams, *The Second Twenty Years at Hull-House, September 1909 to September 1929, with a Record of Growing World Consciousness* (New York: Macmillan, 1930), 47.

16. Addams, *The Second Twenty Years at Hull-House,* 92.

17. Ibid., 110.

18. William James, *Pragmatism* (Cambridge: Harvard University Press, 1975), 35.

19. John Dewey, *Democracy and Education,* included in Dewey, *Middle Works,* vol. 9: *1916,* ed. Jo Ann Boydston (Carbondale: Southern Illinois University Press, 1980), 354.

20. John Dewey, *Experience and Nature,* included in Dewey, *Later Works,* vol. 1: *1925,* ed. Jo Ann Boydston (Carbondale: Southern Illinois University Press, 1981), 141.

21. Addams, *Twenty Years at Hull-House,* 172

22. Jane Addams, "Aspects of the Women's Movement," in *Jane Addams: A Centennial Reader* (New York: Macmillan, 1960), 130.

23. Hans Seigfried, "The Voices of the Victims," in *Contemporary Portraits of Auschwitz: Philosophical Challenges,* ed. A. Rosenberg, J. R. Watson, and D. Linke (New York: Humanity Books, 2000), 43–45.

24. Dewey, *Democracy and Education,* 349.

25. Jane Addams, *The Spirit of Youth and the City Streets* (1909, repr. Urbana: University of Illinois Press, 2001).

26. The Devil Baby episode was also published in the *Atlantic* (Oct. 1916) and later included in *Atlantic Classics,* 2d ser. (Boston: Atlantic Monthly Press, 1918), 52–77 (the editor called it a "contemporary legend") and *The Second Twenty Years at Hull-House,* 49–79. In neither of these other versions did Addams frame it as illustrative of women's memories, as can be seen from the differing opening and concluding paragraphs in each case. The actual incident occurred in 1912 (Addams, *Jane Addams,* 66).

27. John Dewey, *Reconstruction in Philosophy,* included in Dewey, *Middle Works,* vol. 12: *1920,* ed. Jo Ann Boydston (Carbondale: Southern Illinois University Press, 1982), 81. As her last chapter shows, Addams was not completely immune to the new anthropological paradigm that assumed an evolutionary development of the human race, from primitive to advanced.

28. For Addams's use of perplexities as a method of inquiry in her social ethics, see Charlene Haddock Seigfried, Introduction to Jane Addams, *Democracy and Social Ethics* (Urbana: University of Illinois Press, 2002).

29. Dewey, *Reconstruction in Philosophy,* 81.

30. Ibid.

31. Charlene Haddock Seigfried, *William James's Radical Reconstruction of Philosophy* (Albany: State University of New York Press, 1990), 75–97, 103–38.

32. For more on the importance of sympathetic understanding to Addams's philosophy, see Charlene Haddock Seigfried, "Socializing Democracy: Jane Addams and John Dewey," *Philosophy of the Social Sciences* 29 (June 1999): 207–30.

33. In "Women and Internationalism," Addams compares women's revulsion to killing young people—a revulsion stemming from the suffering they would feel if the children they have brought into the world and nurtured were to be killed—to the reluctance an artist would feel if commanded to destroy a great work of art such as the Duomo in Florence. In both cases, she observes that it is a logical step from the intimate experience of cherishing a particular creation of one's own to extending this regard to similar creations of others. Jane Addams, Emily Greene Balch, and Alice Hamilton, *Women at The Hague* (New York: Macmillan, 1915), 128.

34. Bart Schultz, "Comment: The Private and Its Problems—Pragmatism, Pragmatist Feminism, and Homophobia," and Larry A. Hickman, "Making the Family Functional: The Case for Legalized Same-Sex Domestic Partnerships," both in *Philosophy of the Social Sciences* 29 (June 1999): 281–305 and 231–47; Charlene Haddock Seigfried, "Who Cares? Pluralizing Gendered Experiences," in Seigfried, *Pragmatism and Feminism: Reweaving the Social Fabric* (Chicago: University of Chicago Press, 1996), 202–23; Charlene Haddock Seigfried, "Second Sex: Second

Thoughts," in *Hypatia Reborn: Essays in Feminist Philosophy,* ed. Azizah Y. Al-Hibri and Margaret A. Simons (Bloomington: Indiana University Press, 1990), 305–22.

35. Richard Shusterman, *Practicing Philosophy: Pragmatism and the Philosophical Life* (New York: Routledge, 1997), 48.

36. Addams, *The Second Twenty Years at Hull-House,* 49. On the special relationship (lesbian by today's standards) of Addams and Smith, see Stebner, *The Women of Hull House,* 160–66.

37. Seigfried, *Pragmatism and Feminism.*

38. Dewey, *Democracy and Education,* 351, emphasis in the original.

39. Ibid., 350.

40. Dewey, *Reconstruction in Philosophy,* 80–87.

The Long Road
of Woman's Memory

Introduction

For many years at Hull-House I have at intervals detected in certain old people, when they spoke of their past experiences, a tendency to an idealization, almost to a romanticism suggestive of the ardent dreams and groundless ambitions we have all observed in the young when they recklessly lay their plans for the future.

I have, moreover, been frequently impressed by the fact that these romantic revelations were made by old people who had really suffered much hardship and sorrow, and that the transmutation of their experiences was not the result of ignoring actuality, but was apparently due to a power inherent in memory itself.

It was therefore a great pleasure when I found this aspect of memory delightfully portrayed by Sir Gilbert Murray in his life of Euripides. He writes that the aged poet, when he was officially made one of the old men of Athens, declared that he could transmute into song traditional tales of sorrow and wrongdoing because, being long past, they had already become part mystery and part music: "Memory, that Memory who is the Mother of the Muses, having done her work upon them."

Here was an explanation which I might have anticipated; it was the Muses again at their old tricks,—the very mother of them this time,— thrusting their ghostly fingers into the delicate fabric of human experience to the extreme end of life. I had known before that the Muses foregathered with the Spirit of Youth and I had even made a feeble attempt to portray that companionship, but I was stupid indeed not to see that they are equally at home with the aged whose prosaic lives sadly need such interference.

Even with this clue in my hands, so preoccupied are we all with our own practical affairs, I probably should never have followed it, had it not been for the visit of a mythical Devil Baby who so completely filled Hull-House with old women coming to see him, that for a period of six weeks I could perforce do little but give them my attention.

When this excitement had subsided and I had written down the corroboration afforded by their eager recitals in the first two chapters of this book, I might have supposed myself to be rid of the matter, incidentally having been taught once more that, while I may receive valuable suggestions from classic literature, when I really want to learn about life, I must depend upon my neighbors, for, as William James insists, the most instructive human documents lie along the beaten pathway.

The subject, however, was not so easily disposed of, for certain elderly women among these selfsame neighbors disconcertingly took quite another line from that indicated by Euripides. To my amazement, their reminiscences revealed an additional function of memory, so aggressive and withal so modern, that it was quite impossible, living as I was in a Settlement with sociological tendencies, to ignore it.

It was gradually forced upon my attention that these reminiscences of the aged, even while softening the harsh realities of the past, exercise a vital power of selection which often necessitates an onset against the very traditions and conventions commonly believed to find their stronghold in the minds of elderly people. Such reminiscences suggested an analogy to the dreams of youth which, while covering the future with a shifting rose-colored mist, contain within themselves the inchoate substance from which the tough-fibred forces of coming social struggles are composed.

In the light of this later knowledge, I was impelled to write the next two chapters of this book, basing them upon conversations held with various women of my acquaintance whose experience in family relationships or in the labor market had so forced their conduct to a variation from the accepted type that there emerged an indication of a selective groping toward another standard. They inevitably suggested that a sufficient number of similar variations might even, in Memory's leisurely fashion of upbuilding tradition, in the end establish a new norm.

Some of these women, under the domination of that mysterious autobiographical impulse which makes it more difficult to conceal the truth than to avow it, purged their souls in all sincerity and unconsciously made plain the part borne in their hard lives by monstrous social injustices.

These conversations proved to be so illustrative of my second thesis that it seemed scarcely necessary to do more than record them. The deduction was obvious that mutual reminiscences perform a valuable function in determining analogous conduct for large bodies of people who have no other basis for mindedness.

So gradual is this process, so unconsciously are these converts under Memory's gentle coercion brought into a spiritual fellowship, that the social changes thus inaugurated, at least until the reformers begin to formulate them and to accelerate the process through propaganda, take on the aspect of beneficent natural phenomena. And yet, curiously enough, I found that the two functions of Memory—first, its important role in interpreting and appeasing life for the individual, and second its activity as a selective agency in social reorganization—were not mutually exclusive, and at moments seemed to support each other. Certain conversations even suggested that the selective process itself might be held responsible for the softened outlines of the past to one looking back, by the natural blurring of nonessentials and the consequent throwing into high relief of common human experiences.

The insistence of Memory upon the great essentials, even to the complete sacrifice of its inherent power to appease, was most poignantly brought to my attention during two months I spent in Europe in the summer of 1915. Desolated women, stripped by war of all their warm domestic interests and of children long cherished in affectionate solicitude, sat shelterless in the devastating glare of Memory. Because by its pitiless light they were forced to look into the black depths of primitive human nature, occasionally one of these heart-broken women would ignore the strident claims of the present and would insist that the war was cutting at the very taproots of the basic human relations so vitally necessary to the survival of civilization. I cannot hope to have adequately reproduced in Chapter V those conversations which themselves partook of the grim aspect of war.

It was during this cataclysmic summer in Europe that I sometimes sought for a solace, or at least for a source of sanity, by resting my mind on the immemorial monuments of ancient Egypt, from which I had once received an almost mystic assurance of the essential unity of man's age-long spiritual effort. But because such guarding of continuity as Egypt had afforded me had been associated with an unexpected revival of childish recollections, I found that Memory was a chief factor also in this situation. Therefore, in spite of the fact that these reminiscences of my childhood were vividly resuscitated in Egypt by a process which postulates a reversal of the one described in the first two chapters of this book, I venture to incorporate my personal experience in the last chapter. It may suggest one more of our obligations to Memory, that Protean Mother, who first differentiated primitive man from the brute; who makes possible our complicated modern life so daily dependent on the experiences of the past; and upon whom at the present moment is thrust the sole responsibility of guarding, for future generations, our common heritage of mutual good-will.

1

Women's Memories:
Transmuting the Past, as Illustrated
by the Story of the Devil Baby

🖎 Quite as it would be hard for any one of us to select the summer in which he ceased to live that life, so ardent in childhood and early youth, when all the real happenings are in the future, so it must be difficult for old people to tell at what period they began to regard the present chiefly as a prolongation of the past. There is no doubt, however, that such instinctive shiftings and reversals have taken place for many old people who, under the control of Memory, are actually living much more in the past than in the ephemeral present.

It is most fortunate, therefore, that in some subtle fashion these old people, reviewing the long road they have travelled, are able to transmute their own untoward experiences into that which seems to make even the most wretched life acceptable. This may possibly be due to an instinct of self-preservation, which checks the devastating bitterness that would result did they recall over and over again the sordid detail of events long past; it is even possible that those people who were not able thus to inhibit their bitterness have died earlier, for as one old man recently reminded me, "It is a true word that worry can kill a cat."

This permanent and elemental function of Memory was graphically demonstrated at Hull-House during a period of several weeks when we were reported to be harboring within its walls a so-called "Devil Baby."

The knowledge of his existence burst upon the residents of Hull-House one day when three Italian women, with an excited rush through the door, demanded that he be shown to them. No amount of denial convinced them that he was not there, for they knew exactly what he was like with his cloven hoofs, his pointed ears and diminutive tail; the

Devil Baby had, moreover, been able to speak as soon as he was born and was most shockingly profane.

The three women were but the forerunners of a veritable multitude; for six weeks from every part of the city and suburbs the streams of visitors to this mythical baby poured in all day long and so far into the night that the regular activities of the settlement were almost swamped.

The Italian version, with a hundred variations, dealt with a pious Italian girl married to an atheist. Her husband in a rage had torn a holy picture from the bedroom wall saying that he would quite as soon have a devil in the house as such a thing, whereupon the devil incarnated himself in her coming child. As soon as the Devil Baby was born, he ran about the table shaking his finger in deep reproach at his father, who finally caught him and, in fear and trembling, brought him to Hull-House. When the residents there, in spite of the baby's shocking appearance, wishing to save his soul, took him to church for baptism, they found that the shawl was empty and the Devil Baby, fleeing from the holy water, was running lightly over the backs of the pews.

The Jewish version, again with variations, was to the effect that the father of six daughters had said before the birth of a seventh child that he would rather have a devil in the family than another girl, where upon the Devil Baby promptly appeared.

Save for a red automobile which occasionally figured in the story and a stray cigar which, in some versions, the new-born child had snatched from his father's lips, the tale might have been fashioned a thousand years ago.

Although the visitors to the Devil Baby included persons of every degree of prosperity and education, even physicians and trained nurses, who assured us of their scientific interest, the story constantly demonstrated the power of an old wives' tale among thousands of men and women in modern society who are living in a corner of their own, their vision fixed, their intelligence held by some iron chain of silent habit. To such primitive people the metaphor apparently is still the very "stuff of life," or rather no other form of statement reaches them; the tremendous tonnage of current writing for them has no existence. It was in keeping with their simple habits that the reputed presence of the Devil Baby should not reach the newspapers until the fifth week of his sojourn at Hull-House—after thousands of people had already been informed of his whereabouts by the old method of passing news from mouth to mouth.

For six weeks as I went about the house, I would hear a voice at the telephone repeating for the hundredth time that day, "No, there is no such baby"; "No, we never had it here"; "No, he couldn't have seen it for fifty cents"; "We didn't send it anywhere, because we never had it"; "I don't mean to say that your sister-in-law lied, but there must be some mistake"; "There is no use getting up an excursion from Milwaukee, for there isn't any Devil Baby at Hull-House"; "We can't give reduced rates, because we are not exhibiting anything"; and so on and on. As I came near the front door, I would catch snatches of arguments that were often acrimonious: "Why do you let so many people believe it, if it isn't here?" "We have taken three lines of cars to come and we have as much right to see it as anybody else"; "This is a pretty big place, of course you could hide it easy enough"; "What are you saying that for, are you going to raise the price of admission?"

We had doubtless struck a case of what the psychologists call the "contagion of emotion" added to that "aesthetic sociability" which impels any one of us to drag the entire household to the window when a procession comes into the street or a rainbow appears in the sky. The Devil Baby of course was worth many processions and rainbows, and I will confess that, as the empty show went on day after day, I quite revolted against such a vapid manifestation of even an admirable human trait. There was always one exception, however; whenever I heard the high eager voices of old women, I was irresistibly interested and left anything I might be doing in order to listen to them. As I came down the stairs, long before I could hear what they were saying, implicit in their solemn and portentous old voices came the admonition:

> "Wilt thou reject the past
> Big with deep warnings?"

It was a very serious and genuine matter with the old women, this story so ancient and yet so contemporaneous, and they flocked to Hull-House from every direction; those I had known for many years, others I had never known and some whom I had supposed to be long dead. But they were all alive and eager; something in the story or in its mysterious sequences had aroused one of those active forces in human nature which does not take orders, but insists only upon giving them. We had abruptly come in contact with a living and self-assertive human quality!

During the weeks of excitement it was the old women who really seemed to have come into their own, and perhaps the most significant result of the incident was the reaction of the story upon them. It stirred their minds and memories as with a magic touch, it loosened their tongues and revealed the inner life and thoughts of those who are so often inarticulate. They are accustomed to sit at home and to hear the younger members of the family speak of affairs quite outside their own experiences, sometimes in a language they do not understand, and at best in quick glancing phrases which they cannot follow; "More than half the time I can't tell what they are talking about," is an oft-repeated complaint. The story of the Devil Baby evidently put into their hands the sort of material with which they were accustomed to deal. They had long used such tales in their unremitting efforts at family discipline, ever since they had frightened their first children into awed silence by tales of bugaboo men who prowled in the darkness.

These old women enjoyed a moment of triumph—as if they had made good at last and had come into a region of sanctions and punishments which they understood. Years of living had taught them that recrimination with grown-up children and grandchildren is worse than useless, that punishments are impossible, that domestic instruction is best given through tales and metaphors.

As the old women talked with the new volubility which the story of the Devil Baby had released in them, going back into their long memories and urging its credibility upon me, the story seemed to condense that mystical wisdom which becomes deposited in the heart of man by unnoticed innumerable experiences.

Perhaps my many conversations with these aged visitors crystallized thoughts and impressions I had been receiving through years, or the tale itself may have ignited a fire, as it were, whose light illumined some of my darkest memories of neglected and uncomfortable old age, of old peasant women who had ruthlessly probed into the ugly depths of human nature in themselves and others. Many of them who came to see the Devil Baby had been forced to face tragic experiences, the powers of brutality and horror had had full scope in their lives and for years they had had acquaintance with disaster and death. Such old women do not shirk life's misery by feeble idealism, for they are long past the stage of make-believe. They relate without flinching the most hideous experiences: "My face has had this queer twist for now nearly sixty years; I was ten when it got that way, the night after I saw my father do my mother to death with his knife." "Yes, I had fourteen children; only two grew to be men and both of them were killed in the same explosion. I was never sure they brought home the right bodies." But even the most hideous sorrows which the old women related had apparently subsided into the paler emotion of ineffectual regret, after Memory had long done her work upon them; the old people seemed, in some unaccountable way, to lose all bitterness and resentment against life, or rather to be so completely without it that they must have lost it long since.

None of them had a word of blame for undutiful children or heedless grandchildren, because apparently the petty and transitory had fallen away from their austere old age, the fires were burnt out, resentments, hatreds, and even cherished sorrows had become actually unintelligible.

Perhaps those women, because they had come to expect nothing more from life and had perforce ceased from grasping and striving, had obtained, if not renunciation, at least that quiet endurance which allows the wounds of the spirit to heal. Through their stored-up habit of acquiescence, they offered a fleeting glimpse of the translucent wisdom, so often embodied in the old, but so difficult to portray. It is doubtless what Michael Angelo had in mind when he made the Sybils old, what Dante meant by the phrase "those who had learned of life," and the age-worn minstrel who turned into song a Memory which was more that of history and tradition than his own.

In contrast to the visitors to the Devil Baby who spoke only such words of groping wisdom as they were able, were other old women who, although they had already reconciled themselves to much misery, were still enduring more: "You might say it's a disgrace to have your son beat you up for the sake of a bit of money you've earned by scrubbing— your own man is different—but I haven't the heart to blame the boy for doing what he's seen all his life, his father forever went wild when the drink was in him and struck me to the very day of his death. The ugliness was born in the boy as the marks of the Devil was born in the poor child up-stairs."

Some of these old women had struggled for weary years with poverty and much childbearing, had known what it was to be bullied and beaten by their husbands, neglected and ignored by their prosperous children, and burdened by the support of the imbecile and the shiftless ones. They had literally gone "Deep written all their days with care."

One old woman actually came from the poorhouse, having heard of the Devil Baby "through a lady from Polk Street visiting an old friend who has a bed in our ward." It was no slight achievement for the penniless and crippled old inmate to make her escape. She had asked "a young bar-keep in a saloon across the road" to lend her ten cents, offering as security the fact that she was an old acquaintance at Hull-House who could not be refused so slight a loan. She marvelled at some length over the goodness of the young man, for she had not had a dime to spend for a drink for the last six months, and he and the conductor had been obliged to lift her into the street car by main strength. She was naturally much elated over the achievement of her escape. To be sure, from the men's side, they were always walking off in the summer and taking to the road, living like tramps they did, in a way no one from the woman's side would demean herself to do; but to have left in a street car like a lady, with money to pay her own fare, was quite a different matter, although she was indeed "clean wore out" by the effort. However, it was clear that she would consider herself well repaid by a sight of the Devil Baby and that not only the inmates of her own ward, but those in every other ward in the house would be made to "sit up" when she got back; it would liven them all up a bit, and she hazarded the guess that she would have to tell them about that baby at least a dozen times a day.

As she cheerfully rambled on, we weakly postponed telling her there was no Devil Baby, first that she might have a cup of tea and rest, and then through a sheer desire to withhold a blow from a poor old body who had received so many throughout a long, hard life.

As I recall those unreal weeks, it was in her presence that I found myself for the first time vaguely wishing that I could administer comfort by the simple device of not asserting too dogmatically that the Devil Baby had never been at Hull-House.

Our guest recalled with great pride that her grandmother had possessed second sight; that her mother had heard the Banshee three times and that she, herself, had heard it once. All this gave her a certain proprietary interest in the Devil Baby and I suspected she cherished a secret hope that when she should lay her eyes upon him, her inherited gifts might be able to reveal the meaning of the strange portent. At the least, he would afford a proof that her family-long faith in such matters was justified. Her misshapen hands lying on her lap fairly trembled with eagerness.

It may have been because I was still smarting under the recollection of the disappointment we had so wantonly inflicted upon our visitor from the poorhouse that the very next day I found myself almost agreeing with her whole-hearted acceptance of the past as of much more importance than the mere present; at least for half an hour the past seemed endowed also for me with a profounder and more ardent life.

This impression was received in connection with an old woman, sturdy in her convictions, although long since bedridden, who had doggedly refused to believe that there was no Devil Baby at Hull House, unless "herself" told her so. Because of her mounting irritation with the envoys who one and all came back to her to report "they say it ain't there," it seemed well that I should go promptly before "she fashed herself into the grave." As I walked along the street and even as I went up the ramshackle outside stairway of the rear cottage and through the dark corridor to the "second floor back" where she lay in her untidy bed, I was assailed by a veritable temptation to give her a full description of the Devil Baby, which by this time I knew so accurately (for with a hundred variations to select from I could have made a monstrous infant almost worthy of his name), and also to refrain from putting too much stress on the fact that he had never been really and truly at Hull-House.

I found my mind hastily marshalling arguments for not disturbing her belief in the story which had so evidently brought her a vivid interest long denied her. She lived alone with her young grandson, who went to work every morning at seven o'clock and save for the short visits made by the visiting nurse and by kind neighbors, her long day was monotonous and undisturbed. But the story of a Devil Baby, with his existence officially corroborated as it were, would give her a lodestone which would attract the neighbors far and wide and exalt her once more into the social importance she had had twenty-four years before when I had first known her. She was then the proprietor of the most prosperous second-hand store on a street full of them, her shiftless, drinking husband and her jolly, good-natured sons doing exactly what she told them to do. This, however, was long past, for "owing to the drink," in her own graphic phrase, "the old man, the boys, and the business, too, were clean gone" and there was "nobody left but little Tom and me and nothing for us to live on."

I remember how well she used to tell a story when I once tried to collect some folk-lore for Mr. Yeats to prove that an Irish peasant does not lose his faith in the little people nor his knowledge of Gaelic phrases simply because he is living in a city. She had at that time told me a wonderful tale concerning a red cloak worn by an old woman to a freshly dug grave. The story of the Devil Baby would give her material worthy of her powers, but of course she must be able to believe it with all her heart. She could live only a few months at the very best, I argued to myself; why not give her this vivid interest and through it awake those earliest recollections of that long-accumulated folklore with its magic power to transfigure and eclipse the sordid and unsatisfactory surroundings in which life is actually spent? I solemnly assured myself that the imagination of old age needs to be fed and probably has quite as imperious a claim as that of youth, which levies upon us so remorselessly with its "I want a fairy story, but I don't like you to begin by saying that it isn't true." Impatiently I found myself challenging the educators who had given us no pedagogical instructions for the treatment of old age, although they had fairly overinformed us as to the use of the fairy tale with children.

The little room was stuffed with a magpie collection, the usual odds and ends which compose an old woman's treasures, augmented in this case by various articles which a second-hand store, even of the most flourishing sort, could not sell. In the picturesque confusion, if anywhere in Chicago, an urbanized group of the little people might dwell; they would certainly find the traditional atmosphere which they strictly require, marvelling faith and unalloyed reverence. At any rate, an eager old woman aroused to her utmost capacity of wonder and credulity was the very soil, prepared to a nicety, for planting the seed-thought of the Devil Baby. If the object of my errand had been an hour's reading to a sick woman, it would have been accounted to me for philanthropic righteousness, and if the chosen reading had lifted her mind from her bodily discomforts and harassing thoughts so that she forgot them all for one fleeting moment, how pleased I should have been with the success of my effort. But here I was with a story at my tongue's end, stupidly hesitating to give it validity, although the very words were on my lips. I was still arguing the case with myself when I stood on the threshold of her room and caught the indomitable gleam of her eye, fairly daring me to deny the existence of the Devil Baby, her slack dropsical body so responding to her overpowering excitement that for the moment she looked alert in her defiance and positively menacing.

But, as in the case of many another weak soul, the decision was taken out of my hands, my very hesitation was enough, for nothing is more certain than that the bearer of a magic tale never stands dawdling on the door-step. Slowly the gleam died out of the expectant old eyes, the erect shoulders sagged and pulled forward, and I saw only too plainly that the poor old woman had accepted one more disappointment in a life already overflowing with them. She was violently thrown back into all the limitations of her personal experience and surroundings, and that larger life she had anticipated so eagerly was as suddenly shut away from her as if a door had been slammed in her face.

I never encountered that particular temptation again, though she was no more pitiful than many of the aged visitors whom the Devil Baby brought to Hull-House. But, perhaps as a result of this experience, I gradually lost the impression that the old people were longing for a second chance at life, to live it all over again and to live more fully and wisely, and I became more reconciled to the fact that many of them had little opportunity for meditation or for bodily rest, but must keep on working with their toil-worn hands, in spite of weariness or faintness of heart.

The vivid interest of so many old women in the story of the Devil Baby may have been an unconscious, although powerful, testimony that tragic experiences gradually become dressed in such trappings in order that their spent agony may prove of some use to a world which learns at the hardest; and that the strivings and sufferings of men and women long since dead, their emotions no longer connected with flesh and blood, are thus transmuted into legendary wisdom. The young are forced to heed the warning in such a tale, although for the most part it is so easy for them to disregard the words of the aged. That the old women who came to visit the Devil Baby believed that the story would secure them a hearing at home was evident, and as they prepared themselves with every detail of it, their old faces shone with a timid satisfaction. Their features, worn and scarred by harsh living, as effigies built into the floor of an old church become dim and defaced by rough-shod feet, grew poignant and solemn. In the midst of their double bewilderment, both that the younger generation was walking in such strange paths and that no one would listen to them, for one moment there flickered up the last hope of a disappointed life, that it may at least serve as a warning, while affording material for an exciting narrative.

Sometimes in talking to a woman who was "but a hair's breadth this side of the darkness," I realized that old age has its own expression for the mystic renunciation of the world. Their impatience with all non-essentials, the craving to be free from hampering bonds and soft conditions, recalled Tolstoy's last impetuous journey, and I was once more grateful to his genius for making clear another unintelligible impulse of bewildered humanity.

Often, in the midst of a conversation, one of these touching old women would quietly express a longing for death, as if it were a natural fulfillment of an inmost desire, with a sincerity and anticipation so genuine that I would feel abashed in her presence, ashamed to "cling to this strange thing that shines in the sunlight and to be sick with love for it." Such impressions were, in their essence, transitory, but one result from the hypothetical visit of the Devil Baby to Hull-House will, I think, remain: a realization of the sifting and reconciling power inherent in Memory itself. The old women, with much to aggravate and little to soften the habitual bodily discomforts of old age, exhibited an emotional serenity so vast and so reassuring, that I found myself perpetually speculating upon how soon the fleeting and petty emotions which now seem unduly important to us might be thus transmuted; at what moment we might expect the inconsistencies and perplexities of life to be brought under this appeasing Memory with its ultimate power to increase the elements of beauty and significance and to reduce, if not to eliminate, all sense of resentment.

2

Women's Memories:
Reacting on Life, as Illustrated
by the Story of the Devil Baby

During the weeks when the Devil Baby seemed to occupy every room in Hull House, I was conscious that all human vicissitudes are, in the end, melted down into reminiscence, and that a metaphorical statement of the basic experiences which are implicit in human nature itself, however crude in form the story may be, has a singular power of influencing daily living.

At moments we also seemed to glimpse the process through which such tales had been evolved. As our visitors to the Devil Baby came day by day, it gradually became evident that the simpler women were moved not wholly by curiosity, but that many of them prized the story as a valuable instrument in the business of living. From them and from the surprising number of others who had been sent by the aged and the bedridden to secure an exact history and description of the child, the suggestion finally became quite irresistible that such a story, outlining a great abstraction, may once have performed the high service of tradition and discipline in the beginnings of a civilized family life.

The legend exhibited all the persistence of one of those tales which has doubtless been preserved through the centuries because of its taming effects upon recalcitrant husbands and fathers. Shamefaced men brought to Hull-House by their women folk to see the baby, but ill concealed their triumph when there proved to be no such visible sign of retribution for domestic derelictions. On the other hand, numbers of men came by themselves, one group from a neighboring factory on their "own time" offered to pay twenty-five cents, a half dollar, two dollars apiece to see the child, insisting that it must be at Hull House because "the women had seen it."

To my query as to whether they supposed we would, for money, exhibit a poor little deformed baby, if one had been born in the neighborhood, they replied: "Sure, why not?" and "it teaches a good lesson, too," they added as an afterthought, or perhaps as a concession to the strange moral standards of a place like Hull-House. All the members in this group of hard-working men, in spite of a certain swagger towards one another and a tendency to bully the derelict showman, wore a hang-dog look betraying that sense of unfair treatment which a man is so apt to feel when his womankind makes an appeal to the supernatural. In their determination to see the child, the men recklessly divulged much more concerning their motives than they had meant to do. Their talk confirmed my impression that such a story may still act as a restraining influence in the sphere of marital conduct which, next to primitive religion, has always afforded the most fertile field for irrational taboos and savage punishments.

What story could be better than this to secure sympathy for the mother of too many daughters and contumely for the irritated father; the touch of mysticism, the supernatural sphere in which it was placed, would render a man quite helpless.

The story of the Devil Baby, evolved in response to the imperative needs of anxious wives and mothers, recalls the theory that woman first fashioned the fairy story, that combination of wisdom and romance, in an effort to tame her mate and to make him a better father to her children, until such stories finally became a crude creed for domestic conduct, softening the treatment men accorded to women. Because such stories, expressing the very essence of human emotion, did not pretend to imitate the outside of life, they were careless of verisimilitude and absolutely indifferent to the real world. They did, however, meet an essential requirement of the good story, in that they dealt with fundamental experiences.

These first pitiful efforts of women were so widespread and powerful that we have not yet escaped their influence. As subconscious memories, they still cast vague shadows upon the vast spaces of life, shadows that are dim and distorted because of their distant origin. They remind us that for thousands of years women had nothing to oppose against unthinkable brutality save "the charm of words," no other implement with which to subdue the fiercenesses of the world about them. Only through words could they hope to arouse the generosity of strength, to secure a measure of pity for themselves and their children, to so protect the life they had produced that "the precious vintage stored from their own agony" might not wantonly be spilled upon the ground. Possibly the multitude of life's failures, the obscure victims of unspeakable wrong and brutality, have embodied their memories in a literature of their own, of which the story of the Devil Baby is a specimen, crude and ugly in form, as would be inevitable, but still bringing relief to the surcharged heart.

During the weeks that the Devil Baby drew multitudes of visitors to Hull-House, my mind was opened to the fact that new knowledge derived from concrete experience is continually being made available for the guidance of human life; that humble women are still establishing rules of conduct as best they may, to counteract the base temptations of a man's world. I saw a new significance in the fact that thousands of women, for instance, make it a standard of domestic virtue that a man must not touch his pay envelope, but bring it home unopened to his wife. High praise is contained in the phrase, "We have been married twenty years and he never once opened his own envelope," or covert blame in the statement, "Of course he got to gambling; what can you expect from a man who always opens his own pay?

These humble domestic virtues, of which women see the need so much more vividly than men do, have furthermore developed their penalties. The latter, too, are put into aphorisms which, in time, when Memory has done her work upon them, may become legendary wisdom.

Such a penalty was recently illustrated in our neighborhood by the fate of an old man who was found in his room almost starved to death. He was pointed out by many of our neighbors as an example of the inevitable fate of one who deserts his family and therefore, "without a woman to keep him straight," falls into drink and shiftlessness and the endless paths of wrongdoing, so that loneliness and destitution inevitably overtake his old age.

The women were so fatalistically certain of this relation of punishment to domestic sin, of reward to domestic virtue, that when they talked about them, as they so constantly did in connection with the Devil Baby, it often sounded as if they were using the words of a widely known ritual. Among the visitors to the Devil Baby were many for-

eign-born peasant women who, when they had come to America, had
been suddenly subjected to the complicated and constantly changing
environment of city life, and, finding no outlet for many inherited tendencies, might easily have been thrown into that state described by
psychologists as one of "baulked disposition." To them this simple tale,
with its direct connection between cause and effect, between wrong-
doing and punishment, brought soothing and relief, and restored a
shaken confidence as to the righteousness of the universe. They used
the story not only to tame restless husbands, but mothers threatened
their daughters that if they went to dance halls or out to walk with
strange young men, they would be eternally disgraced by devil babies.
As the story grew, the girls themselves seized upon it as a palpable punishment to be held over the heads of reckless friends. That the tale was
useful was evidenced by many letters similar to the anonymous epistle
here given.

> "me and my friends we work in talor shop and when we are going
> home on the roby street car where we get off that car at blue island
> ave. we will meet some fellows sitting at that street where they drink
> some beer from pail. they keep look in cars all time and they will
> wait and see if we will come sometimes we will have to work, but
> they will wait so long they are tired and they dont care they get rest
> so long but a girl what works in twine mill saw them talk with us
> we know her good and she say what youse talk with old drunk man
> for we shall come to thier dance when it will be they will tell us and
> we should know all about where to see them that girl she say oh if
> you will go with them you will get devils baby like some other girls
> did who we knows. she say Jane Addams she will show one like that
> in Hull House if you will go down there we shall come sometime
> and we will see if that is trouth we do not believe her for she is
> friendly with them old men herself when she go out from her work
> they will wink to her and say something else to. We will go down
> and see you and make a lie from what she say."

Because the Devil Baby embodied an undeserved wrong to a poor
mother whose tender child had been claimed by the forces of evil, his
merely reputed presence had power to attract to Hull-House hundreds
of women who had been humbled and disgraced by their children;
mothers of the feeble-minded, of the vicious, of the criminal, of the
prostitute. In their talk it was as if their long rôle of maternal apology

and protective reticence had at last broken down, as if they could speak out freely because for once a man responsible for an ill-begotten child had been "met up with" and had received his deserts. Their sinister version of the story was that the father of the Devil Baby had married without confessing a hideous crime committed years before, thus basely deceiving both his innocent young bride and the good priest who performed the solemn ceremony; that the sin had become incarnate in his child which, to the horror of the young and trusting mother, had been born with all the outward aspects of the devil himself.

As if drawn by a magnet, these forlorn women issued forth from the many homes in which dwelt "the two unprofitable goddesses, Poverty and Impossibility." Occasionally it seemed to me that the women were impelled by a longing to see one good case of retribution before they died, as a bullied child hopes to deal at least one crushing blow at his tormentor when he "grows up," but I think, on the whole, such an explanation was a mistake; it is more probable that the avidity of the women demonstrated that the story itself, like all interpretative art, was "one of those free, unconscious attempts to satisfy, outside of life, those cravings which life itself leaves unsatisfied." At moments, however, baffled desires, sharp cries of pain, echoes of justices unfulfilled, the original material from which such tales are fashioned, would defy Memory's appeasing power and break through the rigid restraints imposed by all Art, even that unconscious of itself.

With an understanding quickened, perhaps, through my own acquaintance with the mysterious child, I listened to many tragic reminiscences from the visiting women; of premature births, "because he kicked me in the side"; of children maimed and burnt because "I had no one to leave them with when I went to work"; women had seen the tender flesh of growing little bodies given over to death because "he wouldn't let me send for the doctor," or because "there was no money to pay for the medicine." But even these mothers, rendered childless through insensate brutality, were less pitiful than some of the others, who might well have cried aloud of their children as did a distracted mother of her child centuries ago:

> "That God should send this one thing more
> Of hunger and of dread, a door
> Set wide to every wind of pain!"

Such was the mother of a feeble-minded boy who said: "I didn't have a devil baby myself, but I bore a poor 'innocent' who made me fight devils for twenty-three years." She told of her son's experiences from the time the other little boys had put him up to stealing that they might hide in safety and leave him to be found with "the goods on him," until grown into a huge man he fell into the hands of professional burglars; he was evidently the dupe and stool-pigeon of the vicious and criminal until the very day he was locked into the State Penitentiary. "If people played with him a little, he went right off and did anything they told him to, and now he's been sent up for life. We call such innocents 'God's Fools' in the old country, but over here the Devil himself gets them. I've fought off bad men and boys from the poor lamb with my very fists; nobody ever came near the house except such-like and the police officers, who were always arresting him."

There were a goodly number of visitors to the Devil Baby of the type of those to be found in every large city, who are on the verge of nervous collapse, or who exhibit many symptoms of mental aberration, and yet are sufficiently normal to be at large most of the time, and to support themselves by drudgery which requires little mental effort, although the exhaustion resulting from the work they are able to do is the one thing from which they should be most carefully protected. One such woman, evidently obtaining inscrutable comfort from the story of the Devil Baby even after she had become convinced that we harbored no such creature, came many times to tell of her longing for her son, who had joined the army eighteen months before and was now stationed in Alaska. She always began with the same words.

"When Spring comes and the snow melts so that I know he could get out, I can hardly stand it. You know I was once in the Insane Asylum for three years at a stretch, and since then I haven't had much use of my mind except to worry with. Of course I know that it is dangerous for me, but what can I do? I think something like this: 'The snow is melting, now he could get out, but his officers won't let him off and if he runs away he'll be shot for a deserter—either way I'll never see him again; I'll die without seeing 'him'—and then I begin all over again with the snow." After a pause, she said: "The recruiting officer ought not to have taken him, he's my only son and I'm a widow. It's against the rules, but he was so crazy to go that I guess he lied a little—at any rate, the government has him now and I can't get him back. Without this worry about him my mind would be all right; if he were here he would be earning money and keeping me and we would be happy all day long."

Recalling the vagabondish lad, who had never earned much money and had certainly never "kept" his hard-working mother, I ventured to suggest that, even if he were at home, he might not have work these hard times, that he might get into trouble and be arrested—I did not need to remind her that he had already been arrested twice—that he was now fed and sheltered and under discipline, and I added hopefully something about his seeing the world. She looked at me out of her withdrawn, harried eyes, as if I were speaking a foreign tongue. "That wouldn't make any real difference to me—the work, the money, his behaving well and all that, if I could cook and wash for him. I don't need all the money I earn scrubbing that factory. I only take bread and tea for supper and I choke over that, thinking of him."

She ceased to speak, overcome by a thousand obscure emotions which could find no outlet in words. She dimly realized that the facts in the case, to one who had known her boy from childhood, were far from creditable, and that no one could understand the eternally unappeased idealism which, for her, surrounded her son's return. She was even afraid to say much about it, lest she should be overmastered by her subject and be considered so irrational as to suggest a return to the Hospital for the Insane.

Those mothers who have never resisted fate nor buffeted against the black waters, but have allowed the waves to close over them, worn and bent as they are by hard labor, subdued and misshapen by the brutality of men, are at least unaffrighted by the melodramatic coarseness of life, which Stevenson more gently describes as "the uncouth and outlandish strain in the web of the world." The story of the Devil Baby may have made its appeal through its frank presentation of this very demoniac quality, to those who live under the iron tyranny of that poverty which threatens starvation, and under the dread of a brutality which may any dark night bring them or their children to extinction; to those who have seen both virtue and vice go unrewarded and who have long since ceased to explain.

This more primitive type embodies the eternal patience of those humble, toiling women who through the generations have been held of little value, save as their drudgery ministered to their men. One of them related her habit of going through the pockets of her drunken son every pay day, and complained that she had never found so little as the night before, only twenty-five cents out of fifteen dollars he had promised for the rent, long overdue. "I had to get that as he lay in the alley before the door; I couldn't pull him in, and the copper who helped him home, left as soon as he heard me coming and pretended he didn't see me. I have no food in the house, nor coffee to sober him up with. I know perfectly well that you will ask me to eat something here, but, if I can't carry it home, I won't take a bite nor a sup. I have never told you so much before. Since one of the nurses said he could be arrested for my non-support, I have been awful close-mouthed. It's the foolish way all the women in our street are talking about the Devil Baby that's loosened my tongue, more shame to me."

A sorrowful woman clad in heavy black, who came one day, exhibited such a capacity for prolonged weeping that it was evidence in itself of the truth of at least half her statement, that she had cried herself to sleep every night of her life for fourteen years in fulfillment of a "curse" laid upon her by an angry man, that "her pillow would be wet with tears as long as she lived." Her respectable husband had a shop in the Red Light district because he found it profitable to sell to the men and women who lived there. She had kept house in the room over the "store" from the time she was a bride newly come from Russia, and her five daughters had been born there, but never a son to gladden her husband's heart.

She took such a feverish interest in the Devil Baby that, when I was obliged to disillusion her, I found it hard to take away her comfort in the belief that the Powers that Be are on the side of the woman when her husband resents too many daughters. But, after all, the birth of daughters was but an incident in her tale of unmitigated woe, for the scoldings of a disappointed husband were as nothing to the curse of a strange enemy, although she doubtless had a confused impression that if there were retribution for one in the general scheme of things, there might be for the other. When the weeping woman finally put the events of her disordered life in some sort of sequence, it became clear that about fifteen years ago she had reported to the police a vicious house whose back door opened into her own yard. Her husband had forbidden her to do anything about it and had said that it would only get them into trouble, but she had been made desperate one day when she saw her little girl, then twelve years old, come out of the door, gleefully showing her younger sister a present of money. Because the poor woman had tried for ten years without success to induce her husband to move from the vicinity of such houses, she was certain that she could save her child only by forcing out "the bad people" from her own door yard. She therefore made her one frantic effort, found her way to the city hall and there reported the house to the chief himself. Of course, "the bad people stood in with the police" and nothing happened to them save, perhaps, a fresh levy of blackmail, but the keeper of the house, beside himself with rage, made the dire threat and laid the curse upon her. In less than a year from that time he had enticed her daughter into a disreputable house in another part of the district. The poor woman, ringing one doorbell after another, had never been able to find her, but her sisters, who in time came to know where she was, had been dazzled by her mode of life. The weeping mother was quite sure that two of her daughters, while still outwardly respectable and "working downtown," earned money in the devious ways which they had learned all about when they were little children, although for the past five years the now prosperous husband had allowed the family to live in a suburb, where the two younger daughters were "growing up respectable."

Certain of the visitors, although confronted by those mysterious and impersonal wrongs which are apparently inherent in the very nature of things, gave us glimpses of another sort of wisdom than that expressed in the assumptions that the decrees of Fate are immutable.

Such a glimpse came to me through a conversation with a woman whose fine mind and indomitable spirit I had long admired; I had known her for years, and yet the recital of her sufferings, added to those the Devil Baby had already induced other women to tell me, pierced me afresh. The story of the Devil Baby may have incited these women to put their experiences more vividly than they had hitherto been able to do. It may have been because they were unconsciously spurred by the hope that a supernatural retribution might intervene even for them, or because they were merely comforted by the knowledge that it had once done so for some one else that they spoke with more confidence than they had ever done before.

"I had eleven children, some born in Hungary and some born here, nine of them boys; all of the children died when they were little but my dear Liboucha. You know all about her. She died last winter in the Insane Asylum. She was only twelve years old when her father, in a fit of delirium tremens, killed himself after he had chased us around the room, trying to kill us first. She saw it all, the blood splashed on the wall stayed in her mind the worst; she shivered and shook all that night through, and the next morning she had lost her voice, couldn't speak out loud for terror. After a while she went to school again and her voice came back, although it was never very natural. She seemed to do as well as ever and was awful pleased when she got into High School. All the money we had I earned scrubbing in a public dispensary, although sometimes I got a little more by interpreting for the patients, for I know three languages, one as well as the other. But I was determined that whatever happened to me, Liboucha was to be educated. My husband's father was a doctor in the old country, and Liboucha was always a clever child. I wouldn't have her live the kind of life I had, with no use for my mind except to make me restless and bitter. I was pretty old and worn out for such hard work, but when I used to see Liboucha on a Sunday morning ready for church in her white dress, with her long yellow hair braided round her beautiful pale face, lying there in bed as I was, being brought up a free-thinker, and needing to rest my aching bones for the next week's work, I'd feel almost happy, in spite of everything. But of course no such peace could last in my life; the second year at High School Liboucha began to seem different and to do strange things. You know the time she wandered away for three days and we were all wild with fright, although a kind woman had taken her in and no harm came to her. I could never be easy after that; she was always gentle, but she was awful sly about running away and at last I had to send her to the asylum. She stayed there off and on for five years, but I saw her every week of my life and she was always company for me, what with sewing for her, washing and ironing her clothes, cooking little things to take out to her, and saving a bit of money to buy fruit for her. At any rate, I had stopped feeling so bitter, and got some comfort out of seeing the one thing that belonged to me on this side of the water, when all of a sudden she died of heart failure and they never took the trouble to send for me until the next day."

She stopped as if wondering afresh that the Fates could have been so casual, but with a sudden illumination, as if she had been awakened out of the burden and intensity of her restricted personal interests into a consciousness of those larger relations that are, for the most part, so strangely invisible. It was as if the young mother of the grotesque Devil Baby, that victim of wrong doing on the part of others, had revealed to this tragic woman much more clearly than soft words had ever done, that the return of a deed of violence upon the head of the innocent is inevitable; as if she had realized that, although she was destined to walk all the days of her life with the piteous multitude who bear the undeserved wrongs of the world, she would walk henceforth with a sense of companionship.

At moments it seemed possible that these simple women, representing an earlier development, eagerly seized upon the story because it was primitive in form and substance. Certainly, one evening, a long-forgotten ballad made an unceasing effort to come to the surface of my mind as I talked to a feeble woman who, in the last stages of an incurable disease from which she soon afterwards died, had been helped off the street car in front of Hull-House. The ballad tells how the lover of a proud and jealous mistress, who demanded as a final test of devotion that he bring her the heart of his mother, had quickly cut the heart from his mother's breast and impetuously returned to his lady, bearing it upon a salver; and how, when stumbling in his gallant haste, he stooped to replace upon the silver plate his mother's heart, which had rolled to the ground, the heart, still beating with tender solicitude, whispered the hope that her child was not hurt. The ballad itself was scarcely more exaggerated than the story of our visitor that evening, who had made the desperate effort of a journey from home in order to see the Devil Baby. I was familiar with her vicissitudes; the shiftless, drinking husband and the large family of children, all of whom had brought her sorrow and disgrace, and I knew that her heart's desire was to see again, before she died, her youngest son, who was a life prisoner in the penitentiary. She was confident that the last piteous stage of her disease would secure him a week's parole, founding this forlorn hope upon the fact that "they sometimes let them out to attend a mother's funeral, and perhaps they'd let Joe come a few days ahead; he could pay his fare afterwards from the insurance money. It wouldn't take much to bury me." Again we went over the hideous story: Joe had violently quarrelled with a woman, the proprietor of the house in which his disreputable wife was living, because she had withheld from him a part of his wife's "earnings," and in the altercation had killed her—a situation, one would say, which it would be difficult for even a mother to condone. But not at all, her thin gray face worked with emotion, her trembling hands restlessly pulled at her shabby skirt as the hands of the dying pluck at their sheets, but she put all the vitality she could muster into his defence. She told us he had legally married the girl, who supported him, "although Lily had been so long in that life that few men would have done it. Of course, such a girl must have a protector or everybody would fleece her. Poor Lily said to the day of her death that he was the kindest man she ever knew, and treated her the whitest; that she herself was to blame for the murder because she told on the old miser, and Joe was so hotheaded she might have known that he would draw a gun for her." The gasping mother concluded: "He was always that handsome and had such a way. One winter, when I was scrubbing in an office building, I'd never get home much before twelve o'clock, but Joe would open the door for me just as pleasant as if he hadn't been waked out of a sound sleep." She was so triumphantly unconscious of the incongruity of a sturdy son in bed while his mother earned his food, that her auditors said never a word, and in silence we saw a hero evolved before our eyes, a defender of the oppressed, the best beloved of his mother, who was losing his high spirits and eating his heart out behind prison bars. He could well defy the world even there, surrounded as he was by that invincible affection which assures both the fortunate and unfortunate alike that we are loved, not according to our deserts, but in response to some profounder law.

This imposing revelation of maternal solicitude was an instance of what continually happened in connection with the Devil Baby. In the midst of the most tragic reminiscences, there remained that something in the memories of these mothers which has been called the great revelation of tragedy, or sometimes the great illusion of tragedy; that which has power in its own right to make life palatable and at rare moments even beautiful.

3

Women's Memories: Disturbing Conventions

✍ In sharp contrast to the function of woman's long memory as a reconciler to life, revealed by the visitors to the Devil Baby, are those individual reminiscences which, because they force the possessor to challenge existing conventions, act as a reproach, even as a social disturber. When these reminiscences, based upon the diverse experiences of many people unknown to each other, point to one inevitable conclusion, they accumulate into a social protest, although not necessarily an effective one, against existing conventions, even against those which are most valuable and those securely founded upon cumulative human wisdom. But because no conventionalized tradition is perfect, however good its intent, most of them become challenged in course of time, unwittingly illustrating the contention that great social changes are often brought about less by the thinkers than by "a certain native and independent rationalism operating in great masses of men and women."

The statement is well founded that a convention is at its best, not when it is universally accepted, but just when it is being so challenged and broken that the conformists are obliged to defend it and to fight for it against those who would destroy it. Both the defenders of an old custom and its opponents are then driven to a searching of their own hearts.

Such searching and sifting is taking place in the consciences of many women of this generation whose sufferings, although strikingly influencing conduct, are seldom expressed in words until they are told in the form of reminiscence after the edges have been long since dulled. Such sufferings are never so poignant as when women have been forced by their personal experiences to challenge the valuable conventions safeguarding family life.

A woman whom I had known slightly for many years came to Hull-House one day escorted by her little grandson. Her delicate features, which were rather hard and severe, softened most charmingly as the little boy raised his cap in good-by from the vanishing automobile. In reply to my admiring comment upon the sturdy lad and his affectionate relation to her, she startled me by saying abruptly, "You know he is really not my grandson. I have scarcely admitted the doubt before, but the time is coming when I must face it and decide his future. If you are kind enough to listen, I want to tell you my experience in all its grim sorrow.

"My husband was shot twenty-seven years ago, under very disgraceful circumstances, in a disreputable quarter of Paris; you may remember something of it in the newspapers, although they meant to be considerate. I was left with my little son, and with such a horror of self-indulgence and its consequences, that I determined to rear my child in strict sobriety, chastity, and self-restraint, although all else were sacrificed to it. Through his school and college days, which I took care should be far from his father's friends and associations, I always lived with him, so bent on rectitude and so distressed by any lack of self-control that I see now how hard and rigorous his life must have been. I meant to sacrifice myself for my child, in reality I sacrificed him to my narrow code.

"The very June that he took his master's degree, I myself found him, one beautiful morning, lying dead in his own room, shot through the temple. No one had heard the report of the revolver, for the little house we had taken was so on the edge of the college town that the neighbors were rather remote, and he must have killed himself while I sat in the moonlight, on the garden bench, after he had left me, my mind still filled with plans for his future.

"I have gone over every word of our conversation that evening in the garden a thousand times; we were planning to come to Chicago for his medical course, and I had expressed my exultant confidence in him to withstand whatever temptation a city might offer, my pride in his purity of thought, his rectitude of conduct. It was then he rose rather abruptly and went into the house to write the letter to me which I found on his table next morning. In that letter he told me that he was too vile to live any longer, that he had sinned not only against his own code of decency and honor, but against my lifelong standards and teachings, and that he realized perfectly that I could never forgive him. He evidently did not expect any understanding from me, either for himself or for 'the young and innocent girl' about to become the mother of his child, and in his interpretation of my rigid morals he was quite sure that I would never consent to see her, but he wrote me that he had told her to send the little baby to me as soon as it was born, obviously hoping that I might be tender to the innocent, although I was so harsh and unpitying to the guilty. I had apparently never given him a glimpse beyond my unbending sternness, and he had all unwittingly pronounced me too self-righteous for forgiveness; at any rate, he faced death rather than my cold disapprobation.

"The girl is still leading the life she had led for two years before my son met her. She is glad to have her child cared for and hopes that I will make him my heir, but understands, of course, that his paternity could never be established in court. So here I am, old and hard, beginning again the perilous experiment of rearing a man child. I suppose it was inevitable that I should hold the girl responsible for my son's downfall and for his death. She was one of the wretched young women who live in college towns for the express purpose of inveigling young men, often deliberately directing their efforts toward those who are reputed to have money. I discovered all sorts of damaging facts about her, which enabled me to exonerate my son from intentional wrong-doing, and to think quite honestly that he had been lured and tempted beyond his strength. The girl was obliged to leave the little town, which was filled with the horror and scandal of the occurrence, but even then, in that first unbridled public censure against the 'bad woman' who had been discovered in the midst of virtuous surroundings, there was a tendency to hold me accountable for my son's death, whatever the girl's earlier responsibility may have been.

"In my loathing of her I experienced all over again the harsh and bitter judgments through which I had lived in the first years after my husband's death. I had secretly held the unknown woman responsible for his end, but of course it never occurred to me to find out about her, and I certainly could never have brought myself to hear her name, much

less to see her. I have at least done better than that in regard to the
mother of my 'grandson,' and Heaven knows I have tried in all humil-
ity and heartbreak to help her. She fairly hated me, as she did anything
that reminded her of my son—the entire episode had seemed to her
so unnatural, so monstrous, so unnecessary—she considered me his
murderer, and I never had the courage to tell her that I agreed with her.
Perhaps if I had done that, really abased myself as I was willing she
should be abased, we might have come into some sort of genuine relation born of our companionship in tragedy. But I couldn't do that,
possibly because the women of my generation cannot easily change the
traditional attitude towards what the Bible calls 'the harlot.' At any rate,
I didn't succeed in 'saving' her. She so obviously dreaded seeing me,
and our strained visits were so unsatisfactory and painful, that I finally gave it up, and her son has apparently quite forgotten her. I am sure
she tries to forget him and all the tragic scenes associated with his earliest babyhood, when I insisted not only upon 'keeping mother and
child together' but also on keeping them with me."

After a moment's pause she resumed: "It would have been compar-
atively easy for me to die when my child was little, when I still had a
right to believe that he would grow up to be a good and useful man,
but I lived to see him driven to his death by my own stupidity. I have
encountered the full penalty for breaking the commandment to judge
not. I passed sentence without hearing the evidence; I gave up the traditional role of the woman who loves and pities and tries to understand;
I forgot that it was my mission to save and not to judge.

"As I have gone back over my unmitigated failure again and again,
I am sure at last that it was the sorry result of my implacable judgment
of the woman I held responsible for my husband's sin. I did not real-
ize the danger nor the inevitable recoil of such a state of self-righteous-
ness upon my child."

As she paused in the recital I rashly anticipated the conclusion, that
her bitter experiences had brought the whole question to that tribu-
nal of personal conduct whose concrete findings stir us to our very
marrow with shame and remorse; that she had frantically striven as we
all do, to keep herself from falling into the pit where the demons of self-
reproach dwell, by clinging to the conventional judgments of the world.
I expected her to set them forth at great length in self-justification, and

perhaps, belonging, as she so obviously did, to an older school, she might even assure me that the wrong to those to whom it was now impossible to make reparation had forever lifted her above committing another such injustice. I found, however, that I was absolutely mistaken and that whatever might be true of her, it still lay within me to commit a gross injustice, when she resumed with these words: "It is a long time since I ceased to urge in my own defence that I was but reflecting the attitude of society, for, in my efforts to get at the root of the matter I have been convinced that the conventional attitude cannot be defended, certainly not upon religious grounds."

She stopped as if startled by her own reflections upon the subject of the social ostracism so long established and so harshly enforced that women seem to hold to it as through an instinct of self-preservation.

She was, perhaps, dimly conscious that the tradition that the unchaste woman should be an outcast from society rests upon a solid basis of experience, upon the long struggle of a multitude of obscure women who, from one generation to another, were frantically determined to establish the paternity of their children and to force the father to a recognition of his obligations; and that the living representatives of these women instinctively rise up in honest rebellion against any attempt to loosen the social control which such efforts have established, bungling and cruel though the control may be.

Further conversation showed that she also realized that these stern memories inherited from the past have an undoubted social value and that it is a perilous undertaking upon which certain women of this generation are bent in their efforts to deal a belated justice to the fallen woman. It involves a clash within the very mass of inherited motives and impulses as well as a clash between old conventions and contemporary principles. On the other hand, it must have been obvious to her in her long effort to get at "the root of the matter" that the punishment and hatred of the bad woman has gone so far as to overreach its own purpose; it has become responsible for such hardness of heart on the part of "respectable" women towards the so-called fallen ones, that punishment is often inflicted not only without regard to justice, but in order to feed the spiritual pride, "I am holier than thou." Such pride erects veritable barricades, deliberately shutting out sympathetic understanding.

The very fact that women remain closer to type than men do and are more swayed by the past, makes it difficult for them to defy settled conventions. It adds to their difficulty that the individual women, driven to modify a harsh convention which has become unendurable to them, are perforce those most sensitive to injustice. The sharp struggle for social advance, which is always a struggle between ideas, long before it becomes embodied in contending social groups, may thus find its arena in the tender conscience of one woman who is pitilessly rent and pierced by her warring scruples and affections. Even such a tentative effort in the direction of social advance exacts the usual toll of blood and tears.

Fortunately the entire burden of the attempt to modify a convention which has become unsupportable, by no means rests solely upon such self-conscious women. Their analytical efforts are steadily supplemented by instinctive conduct on the part of many others. A great mass of "variation from type," accelerating this social change, is contributed by simple mothers who have been impelled by the same primitive emotion which the Devil Baby had obviously released in so many old women. This is an overwhelming pity and sense of tender comprehension, doubtless closely related to the compunction characteristic of all primitive people which in the earliest stage of social development long performed the first rude offices of a sense of justice. This early trait is still a factor in the social struggle, for as has often been pointed out, our social state is like a countryside—of a complex geological structure, with outcrops of strata of very diverse ages.

Such compunction sometimes carries the grandmother of an illegitimate child to the point of caring for the child when she is still utterly unable to forgive her daughter, the child's mother. Even that is a step in advance from the time when the daughter was driven from the house and her child, because a bastard, was conscientiously treated as an outcast both by the family and by the community.

Such an instance of compunction was recently brought to my attention when Hull-House made an effort to place a subnormal little girl twelve years old in an institution in order that she might be protected from certain designing men in the neighborhood. The grandmother who had always taken care of her savagely opposed the effort step by step. She had scrubbed the lavatories in a public building during the twenty-five years of her widowhood, and because she worked all day had been unable to protect her own feeble-minded daughter who, when barely fifteen years old, had become the mother of this child. When her granddaughter was finally placed in the institution, the old woman was absolutely desolated. She found it almost impossible to return home after her day's work because "it was too empty and lonesome, and nothing to come back for. You see," she explained, "my youngest boy wasn't right in his head either and kept his bed for the last fifteen years of his life. During all that time I took care of him the way one does of a baby, and I hurried home every night with my heart in my mouth until I saw that he was all right. He died the year this little girl was born and she kind of took his place. I kept her in a day nursery while she was little, and when she was seven years old the ladies there sent her to school in one of the subnormal rooms and let her come back to the nursery for her meals. I thought she was getting along all right and I took care never to let her go near her mother." The old woman made it quite clear that this was because her daughter was keeping house with a man with whom there had been no marriage ceremony. In her simple code, to go to such a house would be to connive at sin, and while she was grateful that the man had established a control over her daughter which she herself had never been able to obtain, she always referred to her daughter as "fallen," although no one knew better than she how unguarded the girl had been. As I saw how singularly free this mother was from self-reproach and how untouched by any indecisions or remorses for the past, I was once more impressed by the strength of the stout habits acquired by those who early become accustomed to fight off black despair. Such habits stand them in good stead in old age, and at least protect them from those pensive regrets and inconsolable sorrows which inevitably tend to surround whatever has once made for early happiness, as soon as it has ceased to exist.

Many individual instances are found in which a woman, hard pressed by life, includes within her tenderness the mother of an illegitimate child. A most striking example of this came to me through a woman whom I knew years ago when she daily brought her three children to the Hull-House day nursery, obliged to support them by her work in a neighboring laundry because her husband had deserted her. I recall her fatuous smile as she used to say that "Tommy is so pleased to see me at night that I can hear him shout 'Hello, ma' when I am a block away." I had known Tommy through many years; periods of adversity when his father was away were succeeded by periods of fitful prosperity when his father returned from his wanderings with the circus with which "he could always find work," because he had once been a successful acrobat and later a clown, and "so could turn his hand to anything that was needed."

Perhaps it was unavoidable that Tommy should have made his best friends among the warmhearted circus people who were very kind to him after his father's death, and that long before the Child Labor Law permitted him to sing in Chicago saloons, he was doing a successful business singing in the towns of a neighboring state. He was a droll little chap "without any sense about taking care of himself," and in those days his mother not only missed his cheerful companionship but was constantly anxious about his health and morals. When he grew older and became a professional he sent his mother money occasionally, although never very much and never with any regularity. She was always so pleased when it came that the two daughters supporting her with their steady wages were inclined to resent her obvious gratification, as they did the killing of the fatted calf on those rare occasions when the prodigal returned "between seasons" to visit his family.

It is possible that his mother thus early acquired the habit of defending him, the black sheep, against the strictures of the good children who so easily become the self-righteous when they feel "put upon." However that may be, five years ago, after one daughter had been married to a skilled mechanic and the other, advanced to the position of a forewoman, was supporting her mother in the comparative idleness of keeping house for two people in three rooms, a forlorn girl appeared with a note from Tommy asking his mother "to help her out until the kid came and she could work again."

The steady daughter would not permit "such a girl to cross the threshold," and the little household was finally broken up upon the issue. The daughter went to live with her married sister, while the mother, having moved into one room with "Tommy's girl," went back to the laundry in order to support herself and her guest.

The daughters, having impressively told their mother that she could come to live with them whenever she "was willing to come alone," dropped the entire situation. In doing this, they were doubtless instinctively responding to a habit acquired through years of "keeping clear of the queer people father knew in the circus and the saloon crowds always hanging around Tommy," in their secret hope to come to know respectable young men. Conscious that they had back of them the opinion of all righteous people they could not understand why their mother, for the sake of a bad girl, had deserted them in this praiseworthy effort in which hitherto she had been the prime mover.

Tommy had sent his "girl" to his mother on the eve of his departure for "a grand tour to the Klondike region," and since then, almost four years ago, she has heard nothing further from him. During the first half of the time the two women struggled on together as best they could, supporting themselves and the child who was brought daily to the nursery by his grandmother. But the pretty little mother, gradually going back to her old occupation of dancing in the vaudeville, had more and more out-of-town engagements, and while she always divided her earnings with the baby, the grandmother suspected her of losing interest in him, a situation which was finally explained when she confessed that she was about to be married to a cabaret manager who "knew nothing of the past," and to beg that the baby might stay where he was. "Of course, I will pay board for him, but his father can be made to do something, too, if we can only get the law on him."

It was at this point that I had the following conversation with the grandmother, who was shrewd enough to see that the support of the baby was being left upon her hands, and that she could expect help from neither his father nor his mother, although she stoutly refused the advice that the whole matter be taken into the Court of Domestic Relations. "If I could only see Tommy once I think I could get him to help, but I can't find out where he is, and he may not be alive for all I know; he was always that careless about himself. If he put on a new red necktie he'd never know if his bare toes were pushing out of his shoes. He probably didn't get proper clothes for 'the Klondike region' and he may have been frozen to death before this. But whatever has happened to him, I can't let his baby go. I suppose I've learned to think differently about some things after all my years of living with a light-minded husband. Maggie came to see me last week, for she means to be a good daughter. She said that Carrie and Joe were buying a house way out on the West Side, that they were going to move into it this month, and that she and I could have a nice big room together. She said, too, that Carrie would charge only half rate board for me, and would be glad to have my help with her little children, for they both think that nobody has such a way with children as I have. The night before, when she and Carrie were playing with the little boys, they remembered some of the funny songs father used to teach Tommy, and how jolly we all were when he came home good-natured and would stand on his head to make the candy fall out of his pockets. I know the two girls really want me to come back, and that they are often homesick, but when I pointed to the bed where the baby was and asked, 'What about him?' Maggie turned as hard as nails and said as quick as a flash, 'We're all agreed that you'll have to put him in an institution. We'll never have any chance with the nice people in a swell neighborhood like ours if you bring the baby.' She looked real white then, and I felt sorry for her when she said, 'Why, they might even think he was my child, you never can tell,' although she was ashamed of that afterwards and cried a little before she left. She told me that she and Carrie, when they were children, were always talking of what they would do when they got old enough to work, how they would take care of me and move to a part of the city where nobody would know anything about the outlandish way their father and Tommy used to carry on. Of course, it was almost telling me that they didn't want me to come to see them if I kept the baby."

My old friend was quite unable to formulate the motives which underlay her determination, but she implied that clinging to this helpless child was part of her unwavering affection for her son when, without any preamble, she concluded the conversation with the remark, "It's the way I always felt about him," as if further explanation were unnecessary.

It was all doubtless a manifestation of Nature's anxious care—so determined upon survival and so indifferent to morals—that had induced her long devotion to her one child least equipped to take care of himself; and for the same reason the helpless little creature whose existence no one else was deeply concerned to preserve had become so entwined in her affections that separation was impossible.

From time to time a mother goes further than this, in her determination to deal justly with the unhappy situation in which her daughter is placed. When the mother of a so-called fallen girl is of that type of respectability which is securely founded upon narrow precepts, inherited through generations of careful living, it requires genuine courage to ignore the social stigma in order to consider only the moral development of her child, although the result of such courage doubtless minimizes the chagrin and disgrace for the girl herself.

In one such instance the parents of the girl, who had been prevented from marrying her lover because the families on both sides objected to differences of religion, have openly faced the situation and made the baby a beloved member of the household. The pretty young mother arrogates to herself a hint of martyrdom for her faith's sake, but the discipline and responsibility are working wonders for her character. In her hope of earning money enough for two, she has been stirred to new ambition and is eagerly attending a business college. She suffers a certain amount of social ostracism but at the same time her steady courage excites genuine admiration.

In another case a fearless mother exacts seven dollars a week in payment of the board for her daughter and the baby, although the girl earns but eight dollars a week in a cigar factory and buys such clothing for two as she can with the remaining dollar. She admits that it is "hard sledding," but that the baby is "mighty nice." Whatever her state of mind, she evidently has no notion of rebelling against her mother's authority, and is humbly grateful that she was not turned out of doors when the situation was discovered. It is possible that the mother's remorse at her failure to guard her daughter from wrong doing enables her thus grimly to defy social standards which, although they are based upon stern and narrow tenets, nevertheless epitomize the bitter wisdom of generations. Such mothers, overcoming that timidity which makes it so difficult to effect changes in daily living, make a genuine contribution to the solution of the vexed problem.

In spite of much obtuseness on the part of those bound by the iron fetters of convention, these individual cases suggest a practical method of procedure. For quite as pity and fierce maternal affection for their own children drove mothers all over the world to ostracize and cruelly punish the "bad woman" who would destroy the home by taking away the breadwinner and the father, so it is possible that, under the changed conditions of modern life, this same pity for little children, this same concern that, even if they are the children of the outcast, they must still be nourished and properly reared, will make good the former wrongs. There has certainly been a great modification of the harsh judgments meted out in such cases, as women all over the world have endeavored, through the old bungling method of trial and error, to deal justly with individual situations. Each case has been quietly judged by reference to an altered moral standard, for while the ethical code like the legal code stands in need of constant revision, the remodeling of the former is always private, tacit and informal in marked contrast to the public and ceremonious acts of law-makers and judges when the latter is changed.

Such measure of success as the organized Woman's Movement has attained in the direction of a larger justice has come through an overwhelming desire to cherish both the illegitimate child and his unfortunate mother. In addition to that, the widespread effort of modern women to obtain a recognized legal status for themselves and their own children has also been largely dependent upon this desire, at least in the beginnings of the movement. Women slowly had discovered that the severe attitude towards the harlot had not only become embodied in the statutory law concerning her, as thousands of court decisions every day bear testimony, but had become registered in the laws and social customs pertaining to good women as well; the Code Napoleon, which prohibited that search be made for the father of an illegitimate child, also denied the custody of her children to the married mother; those same states in which the laws considered a little girl of ten years the seducer of a man of well-known immorality, did not allow a married woman to hold her own property nor to retain her own wages.

The enthusiasm responsible for the worldwide Woman's Movement was generated in the revolt against such gross injustices. The most satisfactory achievements of the movement have been secured in the Scandinavian countries, where the splendid code of laws protecting all women and children was founded on the instinct to defend the weakest, and upon a determination to lighten that social opprobrium which makes it so unreasonably difficult for a mother to support a child born out of wedlock. In Germany, when the presence of over a million illegitimate children under the age of fourteen years made the situation acute, the best women of the nation, asserting that all attempts to deal out social punishment upon the mothers resulted only in a multitude of ill-nourished and weakened children, founded "The Mutterchutz" Movement. Through its efforts to secure justice and protection for these mothers, it has come to be the great defender of the legal rights of all German women.

Many achievements of the modern movement demonstrate that woman deals most efficiently with fresh experiences when she coalesces them into the impressions Memory has kept in store for her. Eagerly seeking continuity with the past by her own secret tests of affinity, she reinforces and encourages Memory's instinctive processes of selection. If she develops her craving for continuity into a willingness to subordinate a part to the whole and into a sustained and self-forgetful search for congruity and harmony with a life which is greater than hers, she may lift the entire selective process into the realm of Art; at least so far as Art is dependent upon proportion and a so far as beauty hangs upon an ineffable balance between restraint and inclusion

In woman's search for "the eternal moment," balanced independently of time itself because so melted both into memories of the past and into surmises of new beauty for the future of her children's children, she may recognize as one of the universal harmonies the touching devotion of the endless multitude of mothers who were the humble vessels for life's continuance and who carried the burden in safety to the next generation.

Maternal affection and solicitude, in woman's remembering heart, may at length coalesce into a chivalric protection for all that is young and unguarded. This chivalry of women expressing protection for those at the bottom of society, so far as it has already developed, suggests a return to that idealized version of chivalry which was the consecration of strength to the defense of weakness, unlike the actual chivalry of the armed knight who served his lady with gentle courtesy while his fields were ploughed by peasant women misshapen through toil and hunger.

As an example of this new chivalry, the Hungarian women have recently risen in protest against a proposed military regulation requiring that all young women in domestic service, who are living in the vicinity of barracks, be examined each week by medical officers in order to protect the soldiers from disease. The good women in Hungary spiritedly resented the assumption that these girls, simply because they are the least protected of any class in the community, should be subjected to this insult.

An instance of this sort once again illustrates that moral passion is the only solvent for prejudice, and that women have come to feel reproached and disturbed when they ignore the dynamic urgency of memories as fundamental as those upon which prohibitive conventions are based.

4

Women's Memories:
Integrating Industry

✍ If it has always been the mission of literature to translate the particular act into something of the universal, to reduce the element of crude pain in the isolated experience by bringing to the sufferer a realization that his is but the common lot, this mission may have been performed through such stories as that of the Devil Baby for simple, hardworking women who at any given moment compose the bulk of the women in the world.

Certainly some of the visitors to the Devil Baby attempted to generalize and evidently found a certain enlargement of the horizon, an interpretation of life as it were, in the effort. They exhibited that confidence which sometimes comes to the more literate person when, finding himself morally isolated among those hostile to his immediate aims, his reading assures him that other people in the world have thought as he does. Later when he dares to act on the conviction his own experience has forced upon him, he has become so conscious of a cloud of witnesses torn out of literature and warmed into living comradeship, that he scarcely distinguishes them from the like-minded people actually in the world whom he has later discovered as a consequence of his deed.

In some of the reminiscences related by working women I was surprised, not so much by the fact that memory could integrate the individual experience into a sense of relation with the more impersonal aspects of life, as that the larger meaning had been obtained when the fructifying memory had had nothing to feed upon but the harshest and most monotonous of industrial experiences.

I held a conversation with one such woman when she came to confess that her long struggle was over and that she and her sister had at last turned their faces to the poorhouse. She clearly revealed not only that she had caught a glimpse of the great social forces of her day, but that she had had the ability to modify her daily living by what she had perceived.

Perhaps, under the shadow of a tragic surrender, she had obtained a new sense of values, or at least had made up her mind that it was not worth while any longer to conceal her genuine experiences, for she talked more fully of her hard life than I had ever heard her before in the many years I had known her. She related in illuminating detail an incident in her long effort of earning, by ill-paid and unskilled labor, the money with which to support her decrepit mother and her imbecile sister. For more than fifty years she had never for a moment considered the possibility of sending either of them to a public institution, although it had become almost impossible to maintain such a household after the mother, who lived to be ninety-four years old, had become utterly distraught.

She was still sharing her scanty livelihood with the feeble-minded sister, although she herself was unable to do anything but wash vegetables and peel potatoes in a small restaurant of her neighborhood. The cold water necessary to these processes made her hands, already crippled with rheumatism, so bad that on some days she could not hold anything smaller than a turnip, although the other people in the kitchen surreptitiously helped her all they could and the cooks gave her broken food to carry home to the ever hungry sister.

She told of her monotonous years in a box factory, where she had always worked with the settled enmity of the other employees. They regarded her as a pace setter, and she, obliged to work fast and furiously in order to keep three people, and full of concern for her old mother's many unfulfilled needs, had never understood what the girls meant when they talked about standing by each other.

She did not change in her attitude even when she found the price of piece work went down lower and lower, so that at last she was obliged to work overtime late into the night in order to earn the small amount she had previously earned by day. She was seventy years old when the legality of the Illinois Ten Hour Law was contested, and her employer wanted her to testify in court that she was opposed to the law because she could not have supported her old mother all those years unless she had been allowed to work nights. She found herself at last dimly conscious of what it was that her long time enemies, the union girls, had been trying to do, and a subconscious loyalty to her own kind made it impossible for her to bear testimony against them. She did not analyze her motives but told me that, fearing she might yield to her employer's request, in sheer panic she had abruptly left his factory and moved her helpless household to another part of the city on the very day she was expected to appear in court. In her haste she left four days unpaid wages behind her, and moving the family took all the money she had painstakingly saved for the coming winter's coal. She had unknowingly moved into a neighborhood of cheap restaurants, and from that time on she worked in any of them which would employ her until now at last she was too feeble to be of much use to anybody.

Although she had never joined the Union which finally became so flourishing in the box factory she had left, she was conscious that in a moment of great temptation she had refrained from seeking her own advantage at the expense of others. As she bunglingly tried to express her motives, she said: "The Irish—you know I was ten years old when we came over—often feel like that; it isn't exactly that you are sorry after you have done a thing, nor so much that you don't do it because you know you will be sorry afterwards, nor that anything in particular will happen to you if you do it, but that you haven't the heart for it, that it goes against your nature."

When I expressed my admiration for her prompt action she replied: "I have never told this before except to one person, to a woman who was organizing for the garment workers and who came to my house one night about nine o'clock, just as I was having my supper. I had it late in those days because I used to scrub the restaurant floor after everybody left. My sister was asleep back of the stove, I looked sharp not to wake her up and I don't believe the Union woman ever knew that she wasn't just like other people. The organizer was looking for some of the women living in our block who had been taking work from the shops ever since the strike was on. She was clean tired out, and when I offered her a cup of tea she said as quick as a flash, 'You are not a scab, are you?' I just held up my poor old hands before her face, swollen red from scrubbing and full of chilblains, and I told her that I couldn't sew a stitch if my life depended on it.

"When I offered her the second cup of tea—a real educated-looking woman she was, and she must have been used to better tea than mine boiled out of the old tea leaves the restaurant cook always let me bring home—I said to her, 'My hands aren't the only reason I'm not scabbing. I see too much of the miserable wages these women around here get for their sweatshop work, and I've done enough harm already with my pace setting, and my head so full of my poor old mother that I never thought of anybody else.' She smiled at me and nodded her head over my old cracked cup. 'You are a Union woman all right,' she said. 'You have the true spirit whether you carry a card or not. I am mighty glad to have met you after all the scabs I have talked to this day.'"

The old woman repeated the words as one who solemnly recalls the great phrase which raised him into a knightly order, revealing a secret pride in her unavowed fellowship with Trades Unions, for she had vaguely known at the time of the Ten Hour trial that powerful federations of them had paid for the lawyers and had gathered the witnesses. Some dim memory of Irish ancestors, always found on the side of the weak in the unending struggle with the oppressions of the strong, may have determined her action. She may have been dominated by a subconscious suggestion "from the dust that sleeps," a suggestion so simple, so insistent and monotonous that it had victoriously survived its original sphere of conduct.

It was in keeping with the drab colored experiences of her seventy hard years that her contribution to the long struggle should have been one of inglorious flight, nevertheless she had gallantly recognized the Trades Union organizer as a comrade in a common cause. She cherished in her heart the memory of one golden moment when she had faintly heard the trumpets summon her and had made her utmost response.

When the simple story of a lifetime of sacrifice to family obligations and of one supreme effort to respond to a social claim came to an end, I reflected that for more than half a century the narrator had freely given all her time, all her earnings, all her affections, and yet during the long period had developed no habit of self-pity. At a crucial moment she had been able to estimate life, not in terms of her self-immolation but in relation to a hard pressed multitude of fellow workers.

As she sat there, a tall, gaunt woman broken through her devotion, she inevitably suggested the industrial wrongs and oppressions suffered by the women who, forgotten and neglected, perform so much of the unlovely drudgery upon which our industrial order depends. At the moment I could recall only one of her starved ambitions which to my knowledge had ever been attained. When a friend tenderly placed a pair of white satin slippers upon the coffined feet of her old mother who for more than ninety years had travelled a long hard road and had stumbled against many stones, the loving heart of the aged daughter overflowed. "It is herself would know how I prayed for white satin shoes for the burial, thinking as how they might make it up to mother, she who never knew where the next pair was coming from and often had to borrow to go to Mass." I remembered that as my friend and I left the spotless bare room wrapped in the mystery of death and walked back to Hull House together, we passed a little child who proudly challenged our attention to his new shoes, "shiny" in the first moment of joyous possession. We could but recognize the epitome of the hard struggle of the very poor, from the moment they scramble out of their rude cradles until they are lowered into their "partial payment" graves, to keep shoes upon their feet. The rare moments of touching pleasure when the simple desire for "a new pair" is fulfilled are doubtless indicated in the early fairy tales by the rewards of glistening red shoes or glass slippers to the good child; in the religious allegories which turn life itself into one long pilgrimage, by the promises to the faithful that they shall be shod with the sandals of righteousness and to the blessed ones, who having formally renounced the world, forswearing shoes altogether and humbly walking on without them, that their bruised and torn feet shall yet gleam lilywhite on the streets of Paradise.

I suddenly saw in this worn old woman who sat before me, what George Sand described as "a rare and austere production of human suffering" and was so filled with a fresh consciousness of the long barren road travelled by the patient mother and daughter, that it merged into the Via Dolorosa of the Poor of the world. It may have been through this suggestion of an actual street that my memory vividly evoked a group of Russian pilgrims I had once seen in Holy Week as they triumphantly approached Jerusalem. Their heads, garlanded in wild flowers still fresh with early dew, were lifted in joyous singing but their broken and bleeding feet, bound in white cloth and thrust into sandals of stripped bark, were the actual sacrifice they were devoutly offering at the Sepulchre.

As my mind swiftly came back from the blossoming fields of Palestine to the crowded industrial district of Chicago, I found myself recalling a pensive remark made by the gifted Rachel Varnhagen, a century ago. "Careless Fate never requires of us what we are really capable of doing."

This overwhelming sense of the waste in woman's unused capacity came to me again during a Garment Workers' strike, when some of the young women involved were sitting in the very chairs occupied so recently by the visitors to the Devil Baby. They brought a curious reminder of the overworked and heavily burdened mothers who had yet been able to keep the taste of life in their mouths and who could not be overborne, because their endurance was rooted in simple and instinctive human affections. During the long strike these young women endured all sorts of privations without flinching; some of them actual hunger, most of them disapprobation from their families, and all of them a loss of that money which alone could procure for them the American standards so highly prized. Through participation in the strike they all took the risk of losing their positions, and yet, facing a future of unemployment and wretchedness, they displayed a stubborn endurance which held out week after week.

Perhaps because of my recent conversations with old women I received the impression that the very power of resistance in such a socialized undertaking as a strike, presents a marked contrast in both its origin and motives to the traditional type of endurance exercised by the mothers and grandmothers of the strikers or by their acquaintances among domestic women living in the same crowded tenements.

When a mother cares for a sick child for days and nights without relief, the long period of solicitude and dread exhausting every particle of her vitality, her strength is constantly renewed from the vast reservoirs of maternal love and pity whenever she touches the soft flesh or hears the plaintive little voice. But such girls as the strikers represent are steadily bending their energies to loveless and mechanical labor, and are obliged to go on without this direct and personal renewal of their powers of resistance. They must be sustained as soldiers on a forced march are sustained, by their sense of comradeship in high endeavor. Naturally, some of the young working women are never able to achieve this and can keep on with the monotony of factory work only when they persuade themselves that they are getting ready, and have not yet begun their own lives, because real living for them must include a home of their own and children to "do for."

Such unutilized dynamic power illustrates the stupid waste of those impulses and affections, registered in the very bodily structure itself, which are ruthlessly pushed aside and considered of no moment to the work in which so many women are now engaged. My conversations with these girls of modern industry continually filled me with surprise that, required as they are to work under conditions unlike those which women have ever before encountered, they have not only made a remarkable adaptation but have so ably equipped themselves with a new set of motives. The girl who stands on one spot for fifty-six hours each week as she feeds a machine, endlessly repeating the identical motions of her arms and wrists, is much further from the type of woman's traditional activity than her mother who cooks, cleans, and washes for the household. The young woman who spends her time in packing biscuits into boxes which come to her down a chute and are whirled away from her on a miniature trolley, has never even seen how the biscuits are made, for the factory proper is separated from the packing room by a door with the sign "No Admittance." She must work all day without the vital and direct interest in the hourly results of her labors which her mother had.

These girls present a striking antithesis to the visitors to the Devil Baby who in their forlorn and cheerless efforts were merely continuing the traditional struggle against brutality, indifference, and neglect that helpless old people and little children might not be trampled in the dust. For these simple women it is the conditions under which the struggle is waged which have changed, rather than the nature of the contest. Even in this unlovely struggle, the older women utilize well seasoned faculties, in contrast to the newly developed powers required by the multitude of young girls who for the first time in the long history of woman's labor, are uniting their efforts in order to obtain opportunities for a fuller and more normal living. Organizing with men and women of divers nationalities they are obliged to form new ties absolutely unlike family bonds. On the other hand, these girls possess the enormous advantage over women of the domestic type of having experienced the discipline arising from impersonal obligations and of having tasted the freedom from economic dependence, so valuable that too heavy a price can scarcely be paid for it.

This clash between the traditional conception of woman's duty narrowed solely to family obligations and the claims arising from the complexity of the industrial situation, manifests scarcely a suggestion of the latent war so vaguely apprehended from the earliest times as a possibility between men and women. Even the restrained Greeks believed that when the obscure women at the bottom of society could endure no longer and "the oppressed women struck back, it would not be justice which came but the revenge of madness." My own observation has discovered little suggesting this mood, certainly not among the women active in the Labor Movement.

I recall the recent experience of an organizer whom I very much admire for her valiant services in the garment trades and whom I have known from her earliest girlhood. Her character confirms the contention that our chief concern with the past is not what we have done, nor the adventures we have met, but the moral reaction of bygone events within ourselves.

As an orphaned child she had been cared for by two aunts who owned between them a little shop which pretended to be a tailoring establishment, but which in reality was a distributing centre for home work among the Italian women and newly immigrated Russian Jews living in the neighborhood. Her aunts, because they were Americans, superior in education and resources to the humble home workers, by dint of much bargaining both with the wholesale houses from which they procured the garments, and with the foreign women to whom they distributed them, had been able to secure a very good commission. For many years they had made a comfortable living, and in addition had acquired an exalted social position in the neighborhood, for they were much looked up to by those so dependent upon them for work.

Although my friend was expected to help in the shop as much as possible, she was sent regularly to school and had already "graduated from the eighth grade," when a law was passed in the Illinois legislature, popularly known as the Anti-Sweatshop Law, which, within a year, had ruined her aunts' business. After they had been fined in court for violating the law, a case which obtained much publicity because smallpox was discovered in two of the tenement houses in which the home finishers were living, the aunts were convinced that they could not continue to give out work to the Italian and Russian Jewish women. Reluctantly foregoing their commissions they then tried crowding their own house and shop with workers, only to be again taken into court and fined when the inspector discovered their kitchen and bedrooms full of half-finished garments. They both flatly refused to go into a factory to work, and after a futile attempt to revive the tailoring business, never very genuine, they were finally reduced to the dimensions of the tiny shop itself, which, under the new regulations as to light and air could accommodate but three people. My friend was at once taken from school and made one of these ill-paid workers and the little household was held together on the pittance the three could earn.

It was but natural, perhaps, that as these displaced proprietors became poorer they should ever grow more bitter against the reformers and the Trades Unionists who, between them, had secured the "highbrow" legislation which had destroyed their honest business.

The niece was married at eighteen to a clerk in a neighboring department store who worked four evenings a week and every other Sunday in his determination to get on. The bride moved into a more prosperous neighborhood and I saw little of her husband or herself for ten years, during which time they made four payments on the little house they occupied fully three miles from the now abandoned sweat-shop. Her husband worked hard with a consuming desire to rear his children in good surroundings as much as possible unlike the slums, as he somewhat brutally designated the neighborhood of his own youth. Through his unrelieved years in the cheap department store where, however, he had always felt a great satisfaction in being well dressed and had resisted any attempts of his fellow clerks to shorten their preposterous hours by trades-union organization, his health was gradually undermined and he finally developed tuberculosis. He was unable to support his family during the last decade of his life, and in her desperate need my friend went back to the only trade she had, that of finishing garments. During these years, although she sold the little house and placed her boy in a semiphilanthropic institution, she steadily faced the problem of earning insufficient wages for the support of the family, the pang of her failure constantly augmented by the knowledge that, in spite of her utmost efforts, the invalid never received the food and care his condition required. The clothing factory in which she then worked illustrated the lowest ebb in the fortune of the garment workers in American cities when, the sweat shop having been largely eliminated through the efforts of the factory inspectors, the workers from every land were crowded into the hastily organized factories. Separated by their diverse languages and through their long habits of home work, they had become too secretive even to tell one another the amount of wages each was receiving. It was as if the competition had been transferred from the sweat shop contractors to the individual workers themselves, sitting side by side in the same room, and perhaps it was not surprising that the workers felt as if they had been hunted down into their very kitchens and their poverty cruelly exposed to public view.

My friend shared this wretchedness and carried into it the bitterness of her early experience. She says now that she never caught even a suggestion that this might be but a transitional period to a more ordered sort of industrial life.

She did not tell me just when and how she had come to the conclusion that wages must be higher, that legal enactment for better conditions must be supplemented by the efforts of the workers themselves, but it was absolutely clear that she had independently reached that conclusion long before a strike in the clothing industry brought her into contact with the organized Labor Movement. It was certainly not until the year of her husband's death that she became aware of the industrial changes which had been taking place during the twenty-two years since her aunts' business had been ruined.

She was grateful that the knowledge had first come to her through an Italian girl working by her side, for, as she explained, her old attitude toward the "dagoes," as a people to be exploited, had to be thoroughly changed before she could be of much real use in organizing a trade in which so many Italians were engaged. Even during the strike itself, to which she was thoroughly committed, having been convinced both of its inevitability and of the justice of its demands, she resented the fact that the leadership was in the hands of Russian Jews and, secure in her Americanism, she felt curiously aloof from the group with which she was so intimately identified.

A few months after the strike my friend fortunately secured a place in a manufactory of men's clothing, in which there had been instituted a Trade Board for the adjustment of grievances, and where wages and hours were determined by joint agreement. When she was elected to the position of shop representative she found herself in the midst of one of the most interesting experiments being carried on in the United States, not only from the standpoint of labor but from that of applying the principles of representative government in a new field. She felt the stimulus of being a part in that most absorbing of all occupations—the reconstruction of a living world.

One evening, at Hull-House, as she came out of a citizenship class she had been attending, she tried to express some of the implications of the great undertaking in which more than ten thousand clothing employees are engaged. She repeated the statement made by the leader of the class that it was the solemn duty and obligation of the United States not only to keep a republican form of government alive upon the face of the earth and to fulfill the expectations of the founders but to modify and develop that type of government as conditions changed; he had said that the spirit of the New England town meeting might be manifested through a referendum vote in a large city, and that it must find some such vehicle of expression if it would survive under changed conditions. Her eyes were quite shining as she made her application to the experiment being carried on in the great clothing factory, with its many shops and departments unified in mutual effort. Evidently her attention had been caught by the similarity between the town meeting in its relation to a more elaborated form of government and the small isolated sweat-shop such as that formerly managed by her aunts, in its relation to the "biggest clothing factory in the world." She had heard her fellow workers say that the "greenhorn" often found much friendliness in a small shop where his own language was spoken, and where he could earn at least a humble living until he grew accustomed to the habits of a new country, whereas he would have been lost and terrified in a factory. She felt very strongly the necessity of translating this sense of comradeship and friendliness into larger terms, and she believed that it could be done by the united workers.

As she sat by my desk, this woman who had not yet attained her fortieth year looked much older, as if illustrating the saying that hard labor so early robs the poor man of his youth that it makes his old age too long. She seemed to me for the moment to have gathered up in her own experience the transition from old conditions to new and to be standing on the threshold of a great development in the lives of working women.

As if she were conscious that I was recalling her past with which I had been so familiar, she began to speak again. "You know that I have both of my children with me now; the girl graduates from the Normal School in June and hopes to put herself through the University after she has taught for a few years. She reminds me of her father in her anxiety to know people of education, to get on in the world, and I am sure she will succeed. The boy has caught the other motive of pulling up with his own trade and of standing by the organized Labor Movement. Of course, sewing was too dull for him, and besides he grew ambitious to be a machinist when he was in the Industrial School where I put him with such a breaking of the heart when he was only ten years old. He has to admit, however, that even his own Machinists' Union, with its traditional trade agreements and joint boards, is far behind our experiment. He went with me to the banquet on May Day. We had marched through the Loop in celebration of our new agreement and had stirring speeches at the Auditorium in the afternoon, but it was in the evening that we really felt at home with each other. When he saw the tremendous enthusiasm for our beloved leader—my boy, I am sorry to say, is a little inclined to despise foreigners and also tailors because they aren't as big and brawny as the members of his dear Machinists' Union—and really caught some notion of the statesmanlike ability required for the successful management of such a complicated and difficult industrial experiment, and when he realized that the ten per cent increase provided for in the new agreement was to go in greater proportion to those at the lower end of the scale, he suddenly forgot his prejudices and I saw him applauding with his hands and feet as if he had really let loose at last.

"Of course, it hasn't been easy for me even during these later years to keep Helen in school and to support my aunt who is now too old and broken even to keep house for us. But we have got on, and quite aside from everything else I am thankful to have had a small share in this forward step in American democracy—at least, that's what they called it at the banquet," she ended shyly.

The experience of my friend bore testimony that in spite of all their difficulties and handicaps, something of social value is forced out of the very situation itself among that vast multitude of women whose oppression through the centuries has typified a sense of helpless and intolerable wrongs. Many of them, even the older ones, are being made slowly conscious of the subtle and impalpable filaments that secretly bind their experiences and moods into larger relations, and they are filled with a new happiness analogous to that of little children when they are first taught to join hands in ordered play.

Is such enthusiastic participation in organized effort but one manifestation of that desire for liberty and for a larger participation in life, found in great women's souls all over the world?

In pursuance of such a desire the working women have the enormous advantage of constant association with each other, an advantage dimly perceived even by pioneer women two hundred years ago.

The hostesses of the famous drawing-rooms of the eighteenth century laid great stress on human intercourse as the individual's best means of cultivation. Certain French women gave as a *raison d'etre* for their brilliant salons that "people must come together in order to exercise justice," and they became enormously proud of the fact that by the end of the century "all Europe was thrown into a state of agitation if injustice were committed in any corner of it."

This hypothesis was gallantly laid down a hundred years before the industrial revolution which, in its consummation, has congregated millions of women into factories all over the world. These myriad women, most of them young and untrained and all of them working under new industrial conditions, are gradually learning to "exercise justice" if only because they have "come together." Their association has been accomplished under the stress of a common necessity, and they have been tutored in a mass at the hard school of bitter experience.

Were the sheltered drawing-room ladies the forerunners of such contemporary advocates of industrial justice or do we find a better prototype in those simple old women who, having reared their own children and having come to be regarded as a depository for domestic wisdom, dispense sound advice to bewildered mothers which always contains the admonition, "Never be partial to any one of them, always be as just as you know how."

Possibly women's organizations of all types are but providing ever-widening channels through which woman's moral energy may flow, revivifying life by new streams fed in the upper reaches of her undiscovered capacities. In either case, we may predict that to control old impulses so that they may be put to social uses, to serve the present through memories hoarding woman's genuine experiences, may liberate energies hitherto unused and may result in a notable enrichment of the pattern of human culture.

5

Women's Memories:
Challenging War

⟡ I was sharply reminded of an obvious division between high tradition and current conscience in several conversations I held during the great European war with women who had sent their sons to the front in unquestioning obedience to the demands of the State, but who, owing to their own experiences, had found themselves in the midst of that ever-recurring struggle, often tragic and bitter, between two conceptions of duty, one of which is antagonistic to the other.

One such woman*, who had long been identified with the care of delinquent children and had worked for many years towards the establishment of a Children's Court, had asked me many questions concerning the psychopathic clinic in the Juvenile Court in Chicago, comparing it to the brilliant work accomplished in her own city through the cooperation of the university faculty. The Imperial government itself had recently recognized the value of this work and at the outbreak of the war was rapidly developing a system through which the defective child might be discovered early in his school career, and might not only be saved from delinquency but such restricted abilities as he possessed be trained for the most effective use. "Through all these years," she said, "I had grown accustomed to the fact that the government was deeply concerned in the welfare of the least promising child. I had felt my own

---

* The following conversation is a composite made from several talks held with each of two women representing both sides of the conflict. Their opinions and observations are merged into one because in so many particulars they were either identical or overlapping. Both women called themselves patriots, but each had become convinced of the folly of war.

efforts so identified with it that I had unconsciously come to regard the government as an agency for nurturing human life and had apparently forgotten its more primitive functions.

"I was proud of the fact that my son held a state position as professor of Industrial Chemistry in the University, because I knew that the research in his department would ultimately tend to alleviate the harshness of factory conditions, and to make for the well-being of the working classes in whose children I had become so interested.

"When my son's regiment was mobilized and sent to the front I think that it never occurred to me, any more than it did to him, to question his duty. His professional training made him a valuable member of the Aviation Corps, and when, in those first weeks of high patriotism his letters reported successful scouting or even devastating raids, I felt only a solemn satisfaction. But gradually through the months, when always more of the people's food supply and constantly more men were taken by the government for its military purposes, when I saw the state institutions for defectives closed, the schools abridged or dismissed, women and children put to work in factories under hours and conditions which had been legally prohibited years before, when the very governmental officials who had been so concerned for the welfare of the helpless were bent only upon the destruction of the enemy at whatever cost to their fellow-citizens, the State itself gradually became for me an alien and hostile thing.

"In response to the appeal made by the government to the instinct of self-preservation, the men of the nation were ardent and eager to take any possible risks, to suffer every hardship, and were proud to give their lives in their country's service. But was it inevitable, I constantly asked myself, that the great nations of Europe should be reduced to such a primitive appeal? Why should they ignore all the other motives which enter into modern patriotism and are such an integral part of devotion to the state that they must in the end be reckoned with?

"I am sure that I had reached these conclusions before my own tragedy came, before my son was fatally wounded in a scouting aëroplane and his body later thrown overboard into a lonely swamp. It was six weeks before I knew what had happened and it was during that period that I felt most strongly the folly and waste of putting men, trained as my son had been, to the barbaric business of killing. This tendency in my thinking may have been due to a hint he had given me in the very last letter I ever received from him, of a change that was taking place within himself. He wrote that whenever he heard the firing of a huge field-piece he knew that the explosion consumed years of the taxes which had been slowly accumulated by some hard-working farmer or shopkeeper, and that he unconsciously calculated how fast industrial research would have gone forward, had his department been given once a decade the costs of a single day of warfare, with the government's command to turn back into alleviation of industrial conditions the taxes which the people had paid. He regretted that he was so accustomed to analysis that his mind would not let the general situation alone but wearily went over it again and again; and then he added that this war was tearing down the conception of government which had been so carefully developed during this generation in the minds of the very men who had worked hardest to fulfill that conception.

"Although the letter sounded like a treatise on government, I knew there was a personal pang somewhere behind this sombre writing, even though he added his old joking promise that when their fathers were no longer killed in industry, he would see what he could do for my little idiots.

"At the very end of the letter he wrote, and they were doubtless the last words he ever penned, that he felt as if science herself in this mad world had also become cruel and malignant.

"I learned later that it was at this time that he had been consulted in the manufacture of asphyxiating gases, because the same gases are used in industry and he had made experiments to determine their poisonousness in different degrees of dilution. The original investigation with which he had been identified had been carried on that the fumes released in a certain industrial process might be prevented from injuring the men who worked in the factory. I know how hard it must have been for him to put knowledge acquired in his long efforts to protect normal living to the brutal use of killing men. It was literally a forced act of prostitution."

As if to free her son's memory from any charge of lack of patriotism, after a few moments she continued: "These modern men of science are red-blooded, devoted patriots, facing dangers of every sort in mines and factories and leading strenuous lives in spite of the popular conception of the pale anaemic scholar, but because they are equally interested in scientific experiments wherever they may be carried on, they inevitably cease to think of national boundaries in connection with their work. The international mind, which really does exist in spite of the fact that it is not yet equipped with adequate organs for international government, has become firmly established, at least among scientists. They have known the daily stimulus of a wide and free range of contacts. They have become interpenetrated with the human consciousness of fellow scientists all over the world.

"I hope that I am no whining coward—my son gave his life to his country as many another brave man has done, but I do envy the mothers whose grief is at least free from this fearful struggle of opposing ideals and traditions. My old father, who is filled with a solemn pride over his grandson's gallant record and death, is most impatient with me. I heard him telling a friend the other day that my present state of mind was a pure demonstration of the folly of higher education for women; that it was preposterous and more than human flesh could bear to combine an intellectual question on the function of government with a mother's sharp agony over the death of her child. He said he had always contended that women, at least those who bear children, had no business to consider questions of this sort, and that the good sense of his position was demonstrated now that such women were losing their children in war. It was enough for women to know that government waged war to protect their firesides and to preserve the nation from annihilation; at any rate, they should keep their minds free from silly attempts to reason it out. It's all Bertha von Suttner's book and other nonsense that the women are writing, he exploded at the end."

Then as if she were following another line of reminiscence she began again. "My son left behind him a war bride, for he obeyed the admonition of the statesmen, as well as the commands of the military officers in those hurried heroic days. But the hasty wooing betrayed all his ideals of marriage quite as fighting men of other nations did violence to his notions of patriotism, and the recklessness of a destructive air raid outraged his long devotion to science. Of course his child will be a comfort to us and his poor little bride is filled with a solemn patriotism which never questions any aspect of the situation. When she comes to see us and I listen to the interminable talk she has with my father, I am grateful for the comfort they give each other, but when I hear them repeating those hideous stories of the conduct of the enemy which accumulate every month and upon which the war spirit continually feeds itself, I with difficulty refrain from crying out upon them that he whose courage and devotion they praise so loudly would never have permitted such talk of hatred and revenge in his presence; that he who lived in the regions of science and whose intrepid mind was bent upon the conquest of truth, must feel that he had died in vain did he know to what exaggerations and errors the so-called patriotism of his beloved country had stooped.

"I listen to them thinking that if I were either older or younger it would not be so hard for me, and I have an unreal impression that it would have been easier for my son if the war had occurred in the first flush of his adventurous youth. Eager as he had been to serve his country, he would not then have asked whether it could best be accomplished by losing his life in a scouting aeroplane or by dedicating a trained mind to industrial amelioration. He might then easily have preferred the first and he certainly would never have been tormented by doubts. But when he was thirty-one years old and had long known that he was steadily serving his country through careful researches, the results of which would both increase the nation's productivity and protect its humblest citizens, he could not do otherwise than to judge and balance social values. I am, of course, proud of his gallant spirit, that did not for a moment regret his decision to die for his country, but I can make the sacrifice seem in character only when I place him back in his early youth.

"At times I feel immeasurably old, and in spite of my father's contention that I am too intellectual, I am consciously dominated by one of those overwhelming impulses belonging to women as such, irrespective of their mental training, in their revolt against war. After all, why should one disregard such imperative instincts? We know perfectly well that the trend of a given period in history has been influenced by 'habits of preference' and by instinctive actions founded upon repeated and unrecorded experiences of an analogous kind; that desires to seek and desires to avoid are in themselves the very incalculable material by which the tendencies of an age are modified. The women in all the belligerent countries who feel so alike in regard to the horror and human waste of this war and yet refrain from speaking out, may be put-

ting into jeopardy that power inherent in human affairs to right themselves through mankind's instinctive shifting towards what the satis-
factions recommend and the antagonisms repulse. The expression of
such basic impulses in regard to human relationships may be most
important in this moment of warfare which is itself a reversion to primitive methods of determining relations between man and man or nation and nation.

"Certainly the women in every country who are under a profound
imperative to preserve human life, have a right to regard this maternal
impulse as important now as was the compelling instinct evinced by
primitive women long ago, when they made the first crude beginnings
of society by refusing to share the vagrant life of man because they
insisted upon a fixed abode in which they might cherish their children.
Undoubtedly women were then told that the interests of the tribe, the
diminishing food supply, the honor of the chieftain, demanded that
they leave their particular caves and go out in the wind and weather
without regard to the survival of their children. But at the present
moment the very names of the tribes and of the honors and glories
which they sought are forgotten, while the basic fact that the mothers
held the lives of their children above all else, insisted upon staying where
the children had a chance to live, and cultivated the earth for their food,
laid the foundations of an ordered society.

"My son used to say that my scientific knowledge was most irregu-
lar, but profound experiences such as we are having in this war throw
to the surface of one's mind all sorts of opinions and half-formed conclusions. The care for conventions, for agreement with one's friends,
is burned away. One is concerned to express only ultimate conviction
even though it may differ from all the rest of the world. This is true in
spite of the knowledge that every word will be caught up in an atmosphere of excitement and of that nervous irritability which is always
close to grief and to moments of high emotion.

"In the face of many distressing misunderstandings I am certain that
if a minority of women in every country would clearly express their convictions they would find that they spoke not for themselves alone but
for those men for whom the war has been a laceration,—'an abdication
of the spirit.' Such women would doubtless formulate the scruples of
certain soldiers whose 'mouths are stopped by courage,' men who
months ago with closed eyes rushed to the defense of their countries.

"It may also be true that as the early days of this war fused us all into an overwhelming sense of solidarity until each felt absolutely at one with all his fellow countrymen, so the sensitiveness to differences is greatly intensified and the dissenting individual has an exaggerated sense of isolation. I try to convince myself that this is the explanation of my abominable and constant loneliness, which is almost unendurable.

"I have never been a Feminist and have always remained quite unmoved by the talk of the peculiar contribution women might make to the State, but during the last dreadful months, in spite of women's widespread enthusiasm for the war and their patriotic eagerness to make the supreme sacrifice, I have become conscious of an unalterable cleavage between Militarism and Feminism. The Militarists believe that government finally rests upon a basis of physical force, and in a crisis such as this, Militarism, in spite of the spiritual passion in war, finds its expression in the crudest forms of violence.

"It would be absurd for women even to suggest equal rights in a world governed solely by physical force, and Feminism must necessarily assert the ultimate supremacy of moral agencies. Inevitably the two are in eternal opposition.

"I have always agreed with the Feminists that, so far as force plays a great part in the maintenance of an actual social order, it is due to the presence of those elements which are in a steady process of elimination; and of course as society progresses the difficulty arising from woman's inferiority in physical strength must become proportionately less. One of the most wretched consequences of war is that it arrests these beneficent social processes and throws everything back into a coarser mould. The fury of war, enduring but for a few months or years, may destroy slow-growing social products which it will take a century to recreate—the 'consent of the governed,' for instance. . . .

"But why do I talk like this! My father would call it one of my untrained and absurd theories about social progress and the functions of government concerning which I know nothing, and would say that I had no right to discuss the matter in this time of desperate struggle. Nevertheless it is better for me in these hideous long days and nights to drive my mind forward even to absurd conclusions than to let it fall into one of those vicious circles in which it goes round and round to no purpose."

In absolute contrast to this sophisticated, possibly oversophisticated, mother was a simple woman who piteously showed me a piece of shrapnel taken from her son's body by his comrades, which they had brought home to her in a literal-minded attempt at comfort. They had told her that the shrapnel was made in America and she showed it to me, believing that I could at sight recognize the manufactured products of my fellow-countrymen. She apparently wished to have the statement either confirmed or denied, because she was utterly bewildered in her feeling about the United States and all her previous associations with it. In her fresh grief, stricken as she was, she was bewildered by a sudden reversal of her former ideals. Many of her relatives had long ago emigrated to America, including two brothers living in the Western states, whom she had hoped to visit in her old age. For many reasons, throughout her youth and early womanhood, she had thought of that far-away country as a kindly place where every man was given his chance and where the people were all friendly to each other irrespective of the land in which they had been born. To have these same American people send back the ammunition which had killed her son was apparently incomprehensible to her.

She presented, it seemed to me, a clear case of that humble internationalism which is founded not upon theories, but upon the widespread immigration of the last fifty years, interlacing nation to nation with a thousand kindly deeds. Her older brother had a fruit ranch which bordered upon one of those co-operative Italian colonies so successful in California, and he had frequently sent home presents from his Italian neighbors with his own little cargoes. The whole had evidently been prized by his family as a symbol of American good-will and of unbounded opportunity. Her younger brother had attained some measure of success as a contractor in an inland town, and when he had written home of the polyglot composition of the gangs of men upon whose labors his little fortune had been founded, she had taken it as an example of all nationalities and religions working happily together. He had also served one term as mayor, obviously having been elected through his popularity with the same foreign colonies from which his employees had been drawn.

For many reasons therefore she had visualized America as a land in which all nationalities understood each other with a resulting friendliness which was not possible in Europe, not because the people still living in Europe were different from those who had gone to America, but because the latter, having emigrated, had a chance to express their natural goodwill for everybody. The nations at war in Europe suggested to her simple mind the long past days of her grandmother's youth when a Protestant threw stones at a Catholic just because he was "different." The religious liberty in America was evidently confused in her mind with this other liberalism in regard to national differences.

Holding this conception of actual internationalism as it had been evolved among simple people, crude and abortive though it was, she had been much more shocked by the fact that friendly Americans should make ammunition to be used for killing any human being than by the actual war itself, because the war was taking place in Europe, where it was still quite natural for a German to fight against a Frenchman or an Italian against an Austrian.

Her son had been a Socialist and from the discussions he sometimes held with his comrades in her house, she had grown familiar with certain phrases which she had taken literally and in some curious fashion had solemnly come to believe were put into practice in her El Dorado of America.

The arguments I had used so many times with her fellow-countrymen to justify America's sale of ammunition, ponderously beginning with The Hague conventions of 1907, I found useless in the face of this idealistic version of America's good-will.

She was evidently one of those people whose affections go out to groups and impersonal causes quite as much as to individuals, thus often supplementing and enlarging harsh and narrow conditions of living. She certainly obtained a curiously personal comfort out of her idealization of America. Her conversation revealed what I had often vaguely felt before when men as well as women talked freely of the war, that her feelings had been hurt, that her very conception of human nature had received a sharp shock and set-back. To her the whole world and America in particular would henceforth seem less kind and her spirit would be less at home. She was tormented by that ever recurring question which perhaps can never be answered for any of us too confidently in the affirmative, "Is the Universe friendly?" The troubled anguish in her old eyes confirmed her statement that the thought of the multitude of men who were being killed all over the world oppressed her day and night. This old woman had remained faithful to the cause of moral unity and bore her humble testimony to one of the noblest and profoundest needs of the human spirit.

These efforts at spiritual adjustment necessitated by the war are attempted by many people, from the simple souls whose hard-won conceptions of a friendly universe have been brought tumbling about their ears, to the thinking men who are openly disappointed to find civilized nations so irrational. Such efforts are encountered in all the belligerent nations as well as in the neutral ones, although in the former they are often inhibited and overlaid by an overwhelming patriotism. Nevertheless, as I met those women who were bearing their hardships and sorrows so courageously, I often caught a glimpse of an inner struggle, as if two of the most fundamental instincts, the two responsible for our very development as human beings, were at strife with each other. The first is tribal loyalty, such unquestioning acceptance of the tribe's morals and standards that the individual automatically fights when the word comes; the second is woman's deepest instinct, that the child of her body must be made to live.

We are told that the peasants in Flanders, whose fields border upon the very trenches, disconsolately came back to them last Spring and continued to plough the familiar soil, regardless of the rain of shrapnel falling into the fresh furrows; that the wine growers of Champagne last Autumn insistently gathered their ripened grapes, though the bombs of rival armies were exploding in their vineyards; why should it then be surprising that certain women in every country have remained steadfast to their old occupation of nurturing life, that they have tenaciously held to their anxious concern that men should live, through all the contagion and madness of the war fever which is infecting the nations of the earth.

In its various manifestations the struggle in women's souls suggests one of those movements through which, at long historic intervals, the human spirit has apparently led a revolt against itself, as it were, exhibiting a moral abhorrence for certain cherished customs which, up to that time, had been its finest expression. A moral rebellion of this sort was inaugurated three thousand years ago both in Greece and Judea against the old custom of human sacrifice. That a man should slay his own child and stand unmoved as the burning flesh arose to his gods was an act of piety, of courage, and of devotion to ideals, so long as he performed the rite wholeheartedly. But after there had gradually grown up in the minds of men first the suspicion, and then the conviction, that it was unnecessary and impious to offer human flesh as a living sacrifice, courage and piety shifted to the men who refused to conform to this long-established custom. At last both the Greeks and the Jews guarded themselves against the practice of human sacrifice with every possible device. It gradually became utterly abhorrent to all civilized peoples, an outrage against the elemental decencies, a profound disturber of basic human relations. Poets and prophets were moved to call it an abomination; statesmen and teachers denounced it as a hideous barbarism, until now it is so nearly abolished by the entire race that it is no longer found within the borders of civilization and exists to-day only in jungles and hidden savage places.

There are indications that the human consciousness is reaching the same stage of sensitiveness in regard to war as that which has been attained in regard to human sacrifice. In this moment of almost universal warfare there is evinced a widespread moral abhorrence against war, as if its very existence were more than human nature could endure. Citizens of every nation are expressing this moral compunction, which they find in sharp conflict with current conceptions of patriotic duty. It is perhaps inevitable that women should be challenged in regard to it, should be called upon to give it expression in such stirring words as those addressed to them by Romain Rolland, "Cease to be the shadow of man and of his passion of pride and destruction. Have a clear vision of the duty of pity! Be a living peace in the midst of war—the eternal Antigone refusing to give herself up to hatred and knowing no distinction between her suffering brothers who make war on each other."

This may be a call to women to defend those at the bottom of society who, irrespective of the victory or defeat of any army, are ever oppressed and overburdened. The suffering mothers of the disinherited feel the stirring of the old impulse to protect and cherish their unfortunate children, and women's haunting memories instinctively challenge war as the implacable enemy of their age-long undertaking.

6

A Personal Experience
in Interpretative Memory

❧ Several years ago, during a winter spent in Egypt, I found within myself an unexpected tendency to interpret racial and historic experiences through personal reminiscences. I am therefore venturing to record in this closing chapter my inevitable conclusion that a sincere portrayal of a widespread and basic emotional experience, however remote in point of time it may be, has the power overwhelmingly to evoke memories of like moods in the individual.

The unexpected revival in my memory of long-forgotten experiences may have been due partly to the fact that we have so long been taught that the temples and tombs of ancient Egypt are the very earliest of the surviving records of ideas and men, that we approach them with a certain sense of familiarity, quite ready to claim a share in these "family papers and title deeds of the race."

We also consider it probable that these primitive human records will stir within us certain early states of consciousness, having learned, with the readiness which so quickly attaches itself to the pseudoscientific phrase, that every child repeats in himself the history of the race. Nevertheless, what I, at least, was totally unprepared to encounter, was the constant revival of primitive and overpowering emotions which I had experienced so long ago that they had become absolutely detached from myself and seemed to belong to some one else—to a small person with whom I was no longer intimate, and who was certainly not in the least responsible for my present convictions and reflections. It gradually became obvious that the ancient Egyptians had known this small person quite intimately and had most seriously and naïvely set down upon the walls of their temples and tombs her earliest reactions in the presence of death.

At moments my adult intelligence would be unexpectedly submerged by the emotional message which was written there. Rising to the surface like a flood, this primitive emotion would sweep away both the historic record and the adult consciousness interested in it, leaving only a child's mind struggling through an experience which it found overwhelming.

It may have been because these records of the early Egyptians are so endlessly preoccupied with death, portraying man's earliest efforts to defeat it, his eager desire to survive, to enter by force or by guile into the heavens of the western sky, that the mind is pushed back into that earliest childhood when the existence of the soul, its exact place of residence in the body, its experiences immediately after death, its journeying upward, its relation to its guardian angel, so often afforded material for the crudest speculation. In the obscure renewal of these childish fancies, there is nothing that is definite enough to be called memory; it is rather that Egypt reproduces a state of consciousness which has so absolutely passed into oblivion that only the most powerful stimuli could revive it.

This revival doubtless occurs more easily because these early records in relief and color not only suggest in their subject matter that a child has been endowed with sufficient self-consciousness to wish to write down his own state of mind upon a wall, but also because the very primitive style of drawing to which the Egyptians adhered long after they had acquired a high degree of artistic freedom, is the most natural technique through which to convey so simple and archaic a message. The square shoulders of the men, the stairways done in profile, and a hundred other details, constantly remind one of a child's drawings. It is as if the Egyptians had painstakingly portrayed everything that a child has felt in regard to death, and having, during the process, gradually discovered the style of drawing naturally employed by a child, had deliberately stiffened it into an unchanging convention. The result is that the traveller, reading in these drawings which stretch the length of three thousand years, the long endeavor to overcome death, finds that the experience of the two—the child and the primitive people—often become confused, or rather that they are curiously interrelated.

This begins from the moment the traveler discovers that the earliest tombs surviving in Egypt, the mastabas,—which resemble the natural results of a child's first effort to place one stone upon another,—are concerned only with size, as if that early crude belief in the power of physical bulk to protect the terrified human being against all shadowy evils were absolutely instinctive and universal. The mastabas gradually develop into the pyramids, of which Breasted says that "they are not only the earliest emergence of organized men and the triumph of concerted effort, they are likewise a silent, but eloquent, expression of the supreme endeavor to achieve immortality by sheer physical force." Both the mastabas at Sahkara and the pyramids at Gizeh, in the sense of Tolstoy's definition of art as that which reproduces in the spectator the state of consciousness of the artist, at once appeal to the child surviving in every adult, who insists irrationally, after the manner of children, upon sympathizing with the attempt to shut out death by strong walls.

Certainly we can all vaguely remember, when death itself, or stories of ghosts, had come to our intimate child's circle, that we went about saying to ourselves that we were "not afraid," that it "could not come here," that "the door was locked, the windows tight shut," that "this was a big house," and a great deal more talk of a similar sort.

In the presence of these primitive attempts to defeat death, and without the conscious aid of memory, I found myself living over the emotions of a child six years old, saying some such words as I sat on the middle of the stairway in my own home, which yet seemed alien because all the members of the family had gone to the funeral of a relative and would not be back until evening, "long after you are in bed," they had said. In this moment of loneliness and horror, I depended absolutely upon the brick walls of the house to keep out the prowling terror, and neither the talk of kindly Polly, who awkwardly and unsuccessfully reduced an unwieldy theology to child-language, nor the strings of paper dolls cut by a visitor, gave me the slightest comfort. Only the blank wall of the stairway seemed to afford protection in this bleak moment against the formless peril.

Doubtless these huge tombs were built to preserve from destruction the royal bodies which were hidden within them at the end of tortuous and carefully concealed passages; but both the gigantic structures in the vicinity of Memphis, and the everlasting hills, which were later utilized at Thebes, inevitably give the impression that death is defied and shut out by massive defences.

Even when the traveller sees that the Egyptians defeated their object by the very success of the Gizeh pyramids—for when their overwhelming bulk could not be enlarged and their bewildering labyrinths could not be multiplied, effort along that line perforce ceased—there is something in the next attempt of the Egyptians to overcome death which the child within us again recognizes as an old experience. One who takes pains to inquire concerning the meaning of the texts which were inscribed on the inner walls of the pyramids and the early tombs, finds that the familiar terror of death is still there although expressed somewhat more subtly; that the Egyptians are trying to outwit death by magic tricks.

These texts are designed to teach the rites that redeem a man from death and insure his continuance of life, not only beyond the grave but in the grave itself. "He who sayeth this chapter and who has been justified in the waters of Natron, he shall come forth the day after his burial." Because to recite them was to fight successfully against the enemies of the dead, these texts came to be inscribed on tombs, on coffins, and on the papyrus hung around the neck of a mummy. But woe to the man who was buried without the texts: "He who knoweth not this chapter cannot come forth by day." Access to Paradise and all its joys was granted to any one, good or bad, who knew the formula, for in the first stages of Egyptian development, as in all other civilizations, the gods did not concern themselves with the conduct of a man toward other men, but solely with his duty to the gods themselves.

The magic formulae alone afforded protection against the shadowy dangers awaiting the dead man when first he entered the next world and enabled him to overcome the difficulties of his journey. The texts taught him how to impersonate particular gods and by this subterfuge to overcome the various foes he must encounter, because these foes, having at one time been overcome by the gods, were easily terrified by such pretence.

When I found myself curiously sympathetic with this desire "to pretend," and with the eager emphasis attached by the Egyptians to their magic formulae, I was inclined to put it down to that secret sympathy with magic by means of which all children, in moments of rebellion against a humdrum world, hope to wrest something startling and thrilling out of the environing realm of the supernatural; but beyond a kinship with this desire to placate the evil one, to overcome him by mysterious words, I found it baffling to trace my sympathy to a definite experience. Gradually, however, it emerged, blurred in certain details, surprisingly alive in others, but all of it suffused with the selfsame emotions which impelled the Egyptian to write his Book of the Dead.

To describe it as a spiritual struggle is to use much too dignified and definite a term; it was the prolonged emotional stress throughout one cold winter when revival services—protracted meetings, they were then called—were held in the village church night after night. I was, of course, not permitted to attend them, but I heard them talked about a great deal by simple adults and children, who told of those who shouted aloud for joy, or lay on the floor "stiff with power" because they were saved; and of others—it was for those others that my heart was wrung—who, although they wrestled with the spirit until midnight and cried out that they felt the hot breath of hell upon their cheeks, could not find salvation. Would it do to pretend? I anxiously asked myself, why didn't they say the right words so that they could get up from the mourners' bench and sit with the other people, who must feel so sorry for them that they would let them pretend? What were these words that made such a difference that to say them was an assurance of heavenly bliss, but if you failed to say them you burned in hell forever and ever? Was the preacher the only one who knew them for sure? Was it possible to find them without first kneeling at the mourners' bench and groaning? These words must certainly be in the Bible somewhere, and if one read it out loud all through, every word, one must surely say the right words in time; but if one died before one was grown up enough to read the Bible through—to-night, for instance—what would happen then? Surely nothing else could be so important as these words of salvation. While I did not exactly scheme to secure them, I was certainly restrained only by my impotence, and I anxiously inquired from everyone what these magic words might be; and only gradually did this childish search for magic protection from the terrors after death imperceptibly merge into a concern for the fate of the soul.

Perhaps, because it is so impossible to classify one's own childish experiences or to put them into chronological order, the traveller at no time feels a lack of consistency in the complicated attitude toward death which is portrayed on the walls of the Egyptian temples and tombs. Much of it seems curiously familiar; from the earliest times, the Egyptians held the belief that there is in man a permanent element which survives—it is the double, the Ka, the natural soul in contradistinction to the spiritual soul, which fits exactly into the shape of the body but is not blended with it. In order to save this double from destruction, the body must be preserved in a recognizable form.

This insistence upon the preservation of the body among the Egyptians, antedating their faith in magic formulae, clearly had its origin, as in the case of the child, in a desperate revolt against the destruction of the visible man.

Owing to this continued insistence upon corporeal survival, the Egyptians at length carried the art of embalming to such a state of perfection that mummies of royal personages are easily recognized from their likenesses to portrait statues. Such confidence did they have in their own increasing ability to withhold the human frame from destruction that many of the texts inscribed on the walls of the tombs assure the dead man himself that he is not dead, and endeavor to convince his survivors against the testimony of their own senses; or rather, they attempt to deceive the senses. The texts endlessly repeat the same assertion, "Thou comest not dead to thy sepulchre, thou comest living"; and yet the very reiteration, as well as the decorations upon the walls of every tomb, portray a primitive terror lest after all the body be destroyed and the element of life be lost forever. One's throat goes dry over this old fear of death expressed by men who have been so long dead that there is no record of them but this, no surviving document of their once keen reactions to life.

Doubtless the Egyptians in time overcame this primitive fear concerning the disappearance of the body, as we all do, although each individual is destined to the same devastating experience. The memory of mine came back to me vividly as I stood in an Egyptian tomb: I was a tiny child making pothooks in the village school, when one day—it must have been in the full flush of Spring, for I remember the crabapple blossoms—during the afternoon session, the A B C class was told that its members would march all together to the burial of the mother of one of the littlest girls. Of course, I had been properly taught that people went to heaven when they died and that their bodies were buried in the cemetery, but I was not at all clear about it, and I was certainly totally unprepared to see what appeared to be the person herself put deep down into the ground. The knowledge came to me so suddenly and brutally that for weeks afterward the days were heavy with a nameless oppression and the nights were filled with horror.

The cemetery was hard by the schoolhouse, placed there, it had always been whispered among us, to make the bad boys afraid. Thither the A B C class, in awestruck procession, each child carefully holding the hand of another, was led by the teacher to the edge of the open grave and bidden to look on the still face of the little girl's mother.

Our poor knees quaked and quavered as we stood shelterless and unattended by family protection or even by friendly grownups; for the one tall teacher, while clearly visible, seemed inexpressively far away as we kept an uncertain footing on the freshly spaded earth, hearing the preacher's voice, the sobs of the motherless children, and, crowning horror of all, the hollow sound of three clods of earth dropped impressively upon the coffin lid.

After endless ages the service was over and we were allowed to go down the long hill into the familiar life of the village. But a new terror awaited me even there, for our house stood at the extreme end of the street and the last of the way home was therefore solitary. I remember a breathless run from the blacksmith shop, past the length of our lonely orchard until the carriage-house came in sight, through whose wide-open doors I could see a man moving about. One last panting effort brought me there, and after my spirit had been slightly reassured by conversation, I took a circuitous route to the house that I might secure as much companionship as possible on the way. I stopped at the stable to pat an old horse who stood munching in his stall, and again to throw a handful of corn into the poultry yard. The big turkey gobbler who came greedily forward gave me great comfort because he was so absurd and awkward that no one could possibly associate him with anything so solemn as death. I went into the kitchen where the presiding genius allowed me to come without protest although the family dog was at my heels. I felt constrained to keep my arms about his shaggy neck while trying to talk of familiar things—would the cake she was making be baked in the little round tins or in the big square one? But although these idle words were on my lips, I wanted to cry out, "Their mother is dead; whatever, whatever will the children do?" These words, which I had overheard as we came away from the graveyard, referred doubtless to the immediate future of the little family, but in my mind were translated into a demand for definite action on the part of the children against this horrible thing which had befallen their mother.

It was with no sense of surprise that I found this long-forgotten experience spread before my eyes on the walls of a tomb built four thousand years ago into a sandy hill above the Nile, at Assuan. The man so long dead, who had prepared the tomb for himself, had carefully ignored the grimness of death. He is portrayed as going about his affairs surrounded by his family, his friends, and his servants; grain is being measured before him into his warehouse, while a scribe by his side registers the amount; the herdsmen lead forth cattle for his inspection; two of them, enraged bulls, paying no attention to the sombre implication of tomb decoration, lower their huge heads, threatening each other as if there were no such thing as death in the world. Indeed, the builder of the tomb seems to have liked the company of animals, perhaps because they were so incurious concerning death. His dogs are around him, he stands erect in a boat from which he spears fish, and so on from one marvelous relief to another, but all the time your heart contracts for him, and you know that in the midst of this elaborately prepared nonchalance he is miserably terrified by the fate which may be in store for him, and is trying to make himself believe that he need not leave all this wonted and homely activity; that if his body is but properly preserved he will be able to enjoy it forever.

Although the Egyptians, in their natural desire to cling to the familiar during the strange experience of death, portrayed upon the walls of their tombs many domestic and social habits whose likeness to our own household life gives us the quick satisfaction with which the traveller encounters the familiar and wonted in a strange land, such a momentary thrill is quite unlike the abiding sense of kinship which is founded upon the unexpected similarity of ideas, and it is the latter which are encountered in the tombs of the eighteenth century dynasty. The paintings portray a great hall, at the end of which sits Osiris, the god who had suffered death on earth, awaiting those who come before him for judgment. In the center of the hall stands a huge balance in which the hearts of men are weighed, once more reminiscent of a childish conception, making clear that as the Egyptians became more anxious and scrupulous they gradually made the destiny of man dependent upon morality, and finally directed the souls of men to heaven or hell according to their merits.

There is a theory that the tremendous results of good and evil, in the earliest awakening to them, were first placed in the next world by a primitive people sore perplexed as to the partialities and injustices of mortal life. This simple view is doubtless the one the child naturally takes. In Egypt I was so vividly recalled to my first apprehension of it, that the contention that the very belief in immortality is but the postulate of the idea of reward and retribution, seemed to me at the moment a perfectly reasonable one.

The incident of my childhood around which it had formulated itself was very simple. I had been sent with a message—an important commission it seemed to me—to the leader of the church choir that the hymn selected for the doctor's funeral was "How blest the righteous when he dies." The village street was so strangely quiet under the summer sun that even the little particles of dust beating in the hot air were more noiseless than ever before. Frightened by the noonday stillness and instinctively seeking companionship, I hurried toward two women who were standing at a gate talking in low tones. In their absorption they paid no attention to my somewhat wistful greeting, but I heard one of them say with a dubious shake of the head that "he had never openly professed nor joined the church," and in a moment I understood that she thought the doctor would not go to heaven. What else did it mean, that half-threatening tone? Of course the doctor was good, as good as any one could be. Only a few weeks before he had given me a new penny when he had pulled my tooth, and once I heard him drive by in the middle of the night when he took a beautiful baby to the miller's house; he went to the farms miles and miles away when people were sick, and everybody sent for him the minute they were in trouble. How could any one be better than that?

In defiant contrast to the whispering women, there arose in my mind, composed doubtless of various Bible illustrations, the picture of an imposing white-robed judge seated upon a golden throne, who listened gravely to all those good deeds as they were read by the recording angel from his great book, and then sent the doctor straight to heaven.

I dimly felt the challenge of the fine old hymn in its claim of blessings for the righteous, and was defiantly ready at the moment to combat the theology of the entire community. Of my own claim to heaven I was most dubious, and I simply could not bring myself to contemplate the day when my black sins should be read aloud from the big book; but when the claim of reward in the next world for well-doing in this, came to me in regard to one whose righteousness was undoubted, I was eager to champion him before all mankind and even before the judges in the shadowy world to come.

This state of mind, this mood of truculent discussion, was recalled by the wall paintings in the tomb of a nobleman in the Theban hills. In an agonized posture he awaits the outcome of his trial before Osiris. Thoth, the true scribe, records on the wall the just balance between the heart of the nobleman, which is in one pan of the scale, and the feather of truth which is in the other. The noble appeals to his heart, which has thus been separated from him, to stand by him during the weighing and not to bear testimony against him. "Oh, heart of my existence, rise not up against me; be not an enemy against me before the divine powers; thou art my Ka that is in my body, the heart that came to me from my mother." The noble even tries a bribe by reminding the Ka that his own chance of survival is dependent on his testimony at this moment. The entire effort on the part of the man being tried is to still the voice of his own conscience, to maintain stoutly his innocence even to himself.

The attitude of the self-justifying noble might easily have suggested those later childish struggles in which a sense of hidden guilt, of repeated failure in "being good," plays so large a part, and humbles a child to the very dust. That the definite reminiscence evoked by the tomb belonged to an earlier period of rebellion may indicate that the Egyptian had not yet learned to commune with his gods for spiritual refreshment.

Whether it is that the long days and magical nights on the Nile lend themselves to a revival of former states of consciousness, or that I had come to expect landmarks of individual development in Egypt, or, more likely still, that I had fallen into a profoundly reminiscent mood,

I am unable to state; but certainly, as the Nile boat approached nearer to him "who sleeps in Philae," something of the Egyptian feeling for Osiris, the god to whom was attributed the romance of a hero and the character of a benefactor and redeemer, came to me through long-forgotten sensations. Typifying the annual "great affliction," Osiris, who had submitted himself to death, mutilation, and burial in the earth, returned each Spring when the wheat and barley sprouted, bringing not only a promise of bread for the body but healing and comfort for the torn mind; an intimation that death itself is beneficent and may be calmly accepted as a necessary part of an ordered universe.

Day after day, seeing the rebirth of the newly planted fields on the banks of the Nile, and touched by a fresh sense of the enduring miracle of Spring with its inevitable analogy to the vicissitudes of human experience, one dimly comprehends how the pathetic legends of Osiris, by providing the Egyptian with an example for his own destiny, not only opened the way for a new meaning in life, but also gradually vanquished the terrors of death.

Again there came a faint memory of a child's first apprehension that there may be poetry out-of-doors, of the discovery that myths have a foundation in natural phenomena, and at last a more definite reminiscence.

I saw myself a child of twelve standing stock-still on the bank of a broad-flowing river, with a little red house surrounded by low-growing willows on its opposite bank, striving to account to myself for a curious sense of familiarity, for a conviction that I had long ago known it all most intimately, although I had certainly never seen the Mississippi River before. I remember that, much puzzled and mystified, at last I gravely concluded that it was one of those intimations of immortality that Wordsworth had written about, and I went back to my cousin's camp in so exalted a frame of mind that the memory of the evening light shining through the blades of young corn growing in a field passed on the way has remained with me for more than forty years.

Was that fugitive sense of having lived before nearer to the fresher imaginations of the Egyptians, as it is nearer to the mind of a child? and did the myth of Osiris make them more willing to die because the myth came to embody a confidence in this transitory sensation of continuous life?

Such ghosts of reminiscence, coming to the individual as he visits one after another of the marvellous human documents on the banks of the Nile, may be merely manifestations of that new humanism which is perhaps the most precious possession of this generation, the belief that no altar at which living men have once devoutly worshipped, no oracle to whom a nation long ago appealed in its moments of dire confusion, no gentle myth in which former generations have found solace, can lose all significance for us, the survivors.

Is it due to this same humanism that, in spite of the overweight of the tomb, Egypt never appears to the traveller as world-weary, or as a land of the dead? Although the slender fellaheen, whom he sees all day pouring the water of the Nile on their parched fields, use the primitive shaduf of their remote ancestors, and the stately women bear upon their heads waterjars of a shape unchanged for three thousand years, modern Egypt refuses to belong to the past and continually makes the passionate living appeal of those hard-pressed in the struggle for bread.

Under the smoking roofs of the primitive clay houses lifted high above the level of the fields, because resting on the ruins of villages which have crumbled there from time immemorial, mothers feed their children, clutched by the old fear that there is not enough for each to have his portion; and the bleak, barren places quite as the dead are always buried in the desert because no black earth can be spared, and that each new harvest, cut with sickles of a curve already ancient when Moses was born, in spite of its quick ripening, is garnered barely in time to save the laborer from actual starvation.

Certain it is that through these our living brothers, or through the unexpected reactions of memory to racial records, the individual detects the growth within of an almost mystical sense of the life common to all the centuries, and of the unceasing human endeavor to penetrate into the unseen world. These records also afford glimpses into a past so vast that the present generation seems to float upon its surface as thin as a sheet of light which momentarily covers the ocean and moves in response to the black waters beneath it.

Index

Addams, Jane: accomplishments, ix–x; works: "Aspects of the Woman's Movement," xvi; *The Long Road of Woman's Memory,* x–xiii, xvi; *The Second Twenty Years at Hull-House,* xxix–xxx, xxxiii n. 26; *The Spirit of Youth and the City Streets,* x, xviii, 3; *Twenty Years at Hull-House* (Addams), x, xii, xv–xvi; "Women and Internationalism," xxxiii n. 33

aesthetic sociability concept, 9

American Civil Liberties Union (ACLU), ix

American Union Against Militarism, ix

anthropology, evolutionary development and, xxxiii n. 27

Anti-Sweatshop Law, 50–51

art: definition of, 70; function of interpretative, 21

Atlantic, Devil Baby episode in, xxxiii n. 26

ballad, of mother's love, 27

Beauvoir, Simone de, xi

body, preservation of, 73–74

Book of the Dead (Egypt), 72

Breasted (writer), 70

burials: child's memory of, 74–75; shoes for, 47. *See also* Egypt

childhood memories: of death, xxviii, 68, 70–71, 73–75; intimations of immortality in, 78–79; process of, 6

Child Labor Law, 36

children: drawing style of, 69–70; efforts of, to overcome death, 70–72; history repeated in individual, 68; moral judgments of, 76–77; primitive thinking of, xxix; support for defective (troubled), 57–58. *See also* childhood memories; illegitimate children

chivalry, women's, 41–42

Code Napoleon, 40

contagion of emotion, Devil Baby as example of, 9–10, 22–28

criminality, susceptibility to, 22

cultures, ancient/primitive vs. modern, xxix

death: acceptance of, xxix–xxx, 78; childhood memories of, xxviii, 68, 70–71, 73–75; efforts to overcome, 69–74; memory of children's, 11; moral judgments in, 76–77; older people's longing for, 16; pragmatist philosophy's neglect of, xxviii. *See also* burials; Egypt

department stores, organizing in, 51

Devil Baby: confronting belief in, 13–16; contagion of emotion and, 9–10, 22–28; experience generalized from episode of, xxiv–xxv, 43; implications of, xx–xxii, xxv–xxvi, 8–9; influence of, xviii, 27–28; knowledge of existence of, 7–8; role in discipline and tradition, xix–xxi, 10, 17–21; status of viewing, 12–13, 16

Dewey, John: on experience, xx, xxv; on intelligence, xvii; on knowledge, xxx, xxxi; on memory, xviii–xix; on rationalist fallacy, xii; on truth, xv

domestic abuse: folktales as counter to, xxi, 18–19; memory of, 11–12

JANE ADDAMS (1860–1935) was a social activist, a leading Progressive reformer, public speaker, author of many books of social criticism, and an original theorist who contributed to the development of American sociology and pragmatist philosophy. Her feminism, pacifism, and pragmatist experimentalism found concrete expression in the institutions she founded or to which she gave early support, including the Hull-House settlement in Chicago, the National Association for the Advancement of Colored People, the National American Woman Suffrage Association, the American Civil Liberties Union, and the Woman's International League for Peace and Freedom. She was awarded the Nobel Peace Prize in 1931.

CHARLENE HADDOCK SEIGFRIED is a professor of philosophy and American studies and a member of the Women's Studies Committee at Purdue University. She is past president of the Society for the Advancement of American Philosophy, was the John Dewey Lecturer for 1998, and is on the executive board of the Society for the Study of Women Philosophers and a member of the American Philosophical Association Committee on the Status of Women. Among her publications are *William James's Radical Reconstruction of Philosophy, Chaos and Context,* and *Pragmatism and Feminism.* She also edited *Feminist Interpretations of John Dewey* and a special issue on feminism and pragmatism in *Hypatia.*

The University of Illinois Press
is a founding member of the
Association of American University Presses.

———————————————————

University of Illinois Press
1325 South Oak Street
Champaign, IL 61820-6903
www.press.uillinois.edu